# Helping with Handwr

Other titles in the **Key Strategies** series

*Planning Primary Science* by Roy Richardson, Phillip Coote and Alan Wood
*Primary Science A Complete Reference Guide* by Michael Evans
*Physical Education A Practical Guide* by Elizabeth Robertson
*From Talking to Handwriting* by Daphne M Tasker

# Helping with Handwriting

**KS KEY STRATEGIES**

## Key Stages 2 & 3

**Rosemary Sassoon**

JOHN MURRAY

Illustrations by Pat Savage from photographs by the author
Cover illustration by Tom Cross

© Rosemary Sassoon 1994
First published in 1994
by John Murray (Publishers) Ltd
50 Albemarle Street, London W1X 4BD

Material in this book has previously been published in the following titles:
*Helping Your Handwriting* by Rosemary Sassoon, published by E.J. Arnold and Son Ltd; *Helping Your Handwriting Teacher's Book* by Rosemary Sassoon, published by Thomas Nelson and Sons Ltd.

Typeset in Rockwell Regular, Palatino and Sassoon by Litho Link Limited, Welshpool, Powys
Printed in Great Britain by St Edmunsbury Press, Bury St Edmunds, Suffolk
A CIP catalogue record for the book is available from the British Library.
ISBN 0-7195-7135-9

# ■ Contents

Introduction

# Introduction

This book is directed both at teachers and at their pupils. The first two sections concern problems and how to diagnose and deal with them from the teachers' angle. The last two sections, which are photocopiable, provide both illustrations and exercises to help pupils (and teachers) to recognize and retrain postural problems as well as ones concerned with letters.

In principle, diagnosis and remediation are the same for all writers but approaches and indications may differ, as well as the type of difficulties, at different ages. This book is graded from the younger to the older pupils. Sections 1 and 2 are more directed towards the junior school, where the teacher will have the responsibility for diagnosing and remediating problems. Section 3 is aimed more towards secondary pupils who may be able to work out some of their problems for themselves with some guidance and the help of the many illustrations provided.

Teachers should be encouraged to read the whole book because their pupils will vary considerably in their levels and their needs. There are plenty of nine year olds who have mature handwriting and whose personal variations will be at the level of most secondary school pupils. Their written work might even be judged as not very legible because of these variations. At the other extreme, sadly, there are many secondary pupils who still have immature separate letters with an incorrect movement – more expected in seven or eight year olds.

No child willingly has bad handwriting. He or she has either been inadequately or inappropriately taught, or possibly has something physically wrong that needs to be diagnosed. The child is not to blame. It is your job, as the teacher, to learn to diagnose the problem, and explain how it has arisen. The diagnosis and explanation need to be informed, accurate and precise. It is then far more useful than any remedial exercise. It can also be a great relief for children to know that someone understands their precise problem at last. Problems with handwriting are not related to intelligence. To the contrary. It is the early developers, who often teach themselves a visual approximation of letters before they start school, who have the most trouble with many aspects of letters.

As far as the actual handwriting is concerned the issues that need to be assessed, particularly at junior and secondary school entrance, are as follows:

1 The movement, height differentials and spacing of letters.
2 The style or model.
3 Speed.
4 Pupils' posture and penhold.
5 The level of joining.

# 1

# Issues in handwriting

# Handwriting in junior schools

The goals set by the National Curriculum should mean that by the age of seven children have a good grasp of basic letters and should be beginning to join up. This, however, cannot be guaranteed, so what are the most important handwriting issues that face the teacher of a new intake of seven to eight year olds?

Your pupils may have come from different infant schools and are likely to be at different levels of competence, so some means of assessment is needed at school entry. Any problems arising from inappropriate or inadequate teaching need to be dealt with at the first possible moment. There may also be other difficulties such as children who use a style markedly different from the one that your school prescribes. This is a matter that requires a much more flexible attitude. This may not make your life as a teacher any easier, it might, however, make your pupils' handwriting more efficient and less painful, for life.

We need to understand the essentials of handwriting and how the usage of written work has altered in recent years. Attitudes must change in order that all our students should be equipped with fast, efficient and flexible handwriting to enable them to deal with the various tasks that face them at different stages in their education. An efficient handwriting style means one that works for the individual and is not only legible but also consistent and relatively effortless. The old idea that children should always conform to some arbitrarily chosen model and produce uniform and neat handwriting to ornament the school walls must alter. It is time to reach a compromise between the needs of the reader, which have always been considered paramount, and the needs of the writer, that have seldom been considered at all.

# Key Issues

## Movement

Teaching handwriting, in the early stages, consists of training the hand in the movements that produce our letters. The importance of getting things right from the start is essential. All your children should be screened for letters that have an incorrect movement. (The term 'movement of basic letters' describes where the various strokes that make up our letters commence, and in which direction they proceed.) Unfortunately many infant teachers either do not notice, or choose to ignore, letters with an incorrect movement. Maybe they hope that such problems will correct themselves later on. Unfortunately, because of the way that our bodies automate anything to do with a motor skill, such as handwriting, it is increasingly difficult for the writer to alter a movement.

## Height differentials

Where letters have inadequate ascending or descending strokes, or where they are not aligned correctly in relation to each other, the children deserve an explanation as to why it is important for them to change. Some children have never had an adequate demonstration of the different heights of letters. Moreover, because of entrenched ideas in many primary schools, early written tasks have been undertaken without the benefit of even a baseline to aid children in what is a difficult discrimination.

The different heights of letters, and their relation to each other, contribute to the deciphering of mature handwriting. Like any other aspect of personal letters, it is not easy to alter these details. By the time children enter junior school the act of writing is likely to be automated. If they have to stop and think how to change a certain letter in any way they will be consciously thinking of what their hands are doing. This will slow down the writer, and the writing, just when more speed is needed.

## The two sets of letters

Capitals and small letters may still confuse some children. These need explaining in the context of the usage of letters in our writing system. It may be tempting to criticise children for still making such elementary mistakes, but surely the blame lies with those teachers who did not explain matters properly in the first place. It is all too easy to forget these different discriminations that we, as adults, take for granted. Few people can give children a logical or historical explanation of why we, in our writing system, have two sets of letters and it is not for me to give you the answer here. It is clearly explained in most encyclopedia, and this perhaps is the better way to discover this information.

## Word or letter spacing

You may have to undo incorrect teaching here. Children have often been told to use a thumb or finger to space their words. Thumbs grow, however, and writing gets smaller. This mistaken concept seems to linger on in children's minds and word spaces become wider and wider, leaving rivers of white down the page. Luckily most children are familiar with keyboards today, so it is only a matter of explaining that a word space is the same as a letter of the same size as the writing.

The direction of writing and mirror image, two other problems caused by our writing system, often worry younger children. These problems should have sorted themselves out by junior school entrance. Where they still cause confusion, clear explanations and exercises are needed. Such problems do not constitute dyslexia, but are more likely to have been caused by inadequate teaching.

# Different handwriting models

This is difficult to explain without sounding as if I am defending bad handwriting. Our country, unlike most others, has a long tradition of respecting individual schools' right to choose their own handwriting model. This concept, much to my relief, is central to our new National Curriculum. I find it interesting, as I observe handwriting around the world, to discover that several countries, where previously national models were enforced, have had to revise their curricula. They have found that their pupils frequently could not speed up their writing in secondary school, and reverted to separate letters. In some cases this was because they had been teaching the old-fashioned continuous cursive which is notoriously difficult to speed up. There is, however, an additional factor involved. When any model is kept for too long or taught too strictly, young writers do not have the opportunity to experiment. Experimentation leads to personal letters, and to the establishment of the slant and proportion that suits individual hands and characters. This is the way to automated and consistent handwriting when the pupil need not worry about adhering to the details of a taught model, but can concentrate on the content of the written work. A more liberal attitude to the model does not necessarily lead to untidy or illegible handwriting, it should lead to the personal shortcuts that result in an efficient, mature hand.

Maybe a model is necessary in the early stages, but what model, and should it be the same for all children? The problem with a national model, or even a strict school model, is that the emphasis inevitably falls on the copying of the details of the model rather than the automation of consistent personal handwriting. Let us be honest. It is far easier to teach children to conform to a strict model. Their work looks more attractive when put up on display. But is it the way for pupils to acquire the fast efficient handwriting that they need today? Flexible and informed teaching is needed to guide pupils at a vulnerable age.

I speak with some feeling on this subject. Of those who come to me with so-called handwriting problems, I often see children who have been forced to alter from a perfectly adequate style of handwriting to that approved by a new school, or to conform to letterforms that are patently unsuitable for them. Some such pupils find it almost impossible to alter their handwriting, and all would be considerably slowed down by having to attend to the form of their letters rather than the content. Some of the most guilty schools have won national competitions, perhaps for the italic handwriting of one or two of their star pupils, which is more like calligraphy than the fast efficient handwriting so desperately needed by high-achieving students.

It may be satisfying for some to control a class by strictly enforcing a model, but what is it doing to the children? It may destroy creativity in written work or produce reluctant writers, often afraid to put pen to paper for fear of the criticism or ridicule that they may face. Some of you may find my comments disturbing, but it is important for you to understand the damaging effects a handwriting model can have, on newcomers to your school in particular. If you are confident that the model that you are teaching is really beneficial, then it is likely that newcomers will come to appreciate this, and gradually alter. If they choose not to alter, then it is not right to force them.

# Speed

At each level of education there is a need to speed up handwriting. Speed is likely to affect neatness at any level, so this needs to be understood by all concerned. When children first enter your school the speeding up may be almost imperceptible, but different written tasks will soon be introduced and it is important that children understand that there are different levels of writing suitable for different tasks. It could be said that to spend time raising handwriting to an unnecessarily high level for any particular task is a waste of time. Most intelligent adults work on that principle automatically, but what does it mean to the average schoolchild? It means that first drafts of essays or notes can be roughly written as long as they are decipherable to the writer, but French homework, for instance, will need even more care than an English exercise, because so much depends on the accuracy of single letters.

Speed tests of the informal kind are useful in encouraging children to keep their pens on the paper and to join up their letters. Later they help pupils to bring out the most efficient joins and individual shortcuts in their personal handwriting. An informed teacher can be crucial in interpreting such experiments. It is often possible to show how a rough scribble is the beginning of mature handwriting, and far better than tight, neat but childish letterforms that still adher to the taught model. The teacher's most important responsibility is to equip their pupils, by whatever means, with a fast enough hand to deal with the next stage of education. Some pupils reject the beginnings of a joined hand because they see it as untidy. Teachers can explain the advantages of joining and help them to develop a fast efficient movement.

When children start secondary school they will need really fast handwriting for note-taking and increased homework. It could all be summed up by saying that a scribble is as vital as slow, neat handwriting, and those pupils who demonstrate the most difference between their levels of handwriting indicate that they are the most flexible and efficient.

# ■ Writing posture

So far the letters have been emphasised but it is also important to consider the writer's body. Have you ever walked behind the rows of desks and observed the tortured postures of so many of your pupils when they are engrossed in their work? Why do we allow this? Why do the children themselves not complain because surely it cannot benefit either the taking in of information or the writing down of it to be so uncomfortable?

## School furniture

Surely children have the right to be appropriately seated to work in the classroom. Relating furniture to posture, and posture to handwriting, it becomes clear that it may not be possible to write well unless the body is properly placed and the arm able to move freely. I can sympathise with schools with overstretched budgets, or those whose furniture purchases are dictated by central buying. However, they should be able to organise matters so that the few over-large, or very small pupils have provision made for them. It is often only a matter of being flexible about the use of the different sizes of furniture that are usually to be found in different parts of most schools. I have seen patients whose health and physiques have been damaged by the extended use of inappropriate furniture in their junior schools. Their bodies, too flexible to feel pain, the body's warning system, became twisted instead. On the other hand, I have seen enlightened schools, where three sizes of chairs and desks are ranged from the back to the front of the class, allowing for the different builds of their pupils.

Writing posture consists of more than sitting posture and desk or chair height. It concerns penhold and also paper position. If children are to be able to hold the pen comfortably, yet still see what they are doing, they need to be taught to place the paper to the side of the hand that writes. Right-handers must place the paper to their right side and left-handers, even more importantly, to their left. This brings us back to furniture because it means that there must be enough space on the desk or table to make this possible. The 'modern' hexagonal tables, which are widely used in infant schools, provide only enough space for the paper to be centrally placed in front of each young writer. This space is so limited that there is not enough room for children to use their other hand to support the paper. You may have to explain this to some of your children and encourage them to alter their paper position so they can sit comfortably, hold their pens happily, and see what they are writing. Even this seemingly simple and beneficial alteration is not always easy. Every aspect of the physical act of writing becomes automated and difficult to change. Without motivation, changes such as those involving paper position or penhold, for instance, may be almost impossible for a pupil who has written in a particular way for several years.

## Pen and penhold

This is an emotive and often explosive subject in some classrooms. First there is the writing implement itself to consider. Pen and penhold are interrelated, as well as the resulting letterforms. Throughout history, as pens developed and letterforms altered in consequence, the writing masters of the day paid attention at each stage to different ways of holding the pen. In the last few decades radical alterations have taken place in the design of pens, yet no one has considered that we ought to develop another penhold. This is one area that I have researched quite thoroughly, and although many of you may not agree with me, I would ask you to start observing your pupils and questioning them, too. After analysing the penholds of several hundred children in detail several points become obvious. First of all, the results showed that unconventional penholds produced faster writing than the more traditional penholds. This certainly needed further investigation, and scrutiny of the photographs of all the writers gave me the answer. Ballpoints were used in my study and much of the distortion of the fingers seemed to be directed at forcing the pen into an upright position in order to function. When you start to think about it, all types of modern pens need to be held in a much more upright position than traditional fountain pens.

I can almost hear those schools who insist on all their pupils using fountain pens, congratulating themselves. But I am afraid that they are the next in the line of fire. I do not believe in making all children use the same writing implement, and if it should be necessary to do so, it would not necessarily be a fountain pen that I would prescribe. Modern pens are here to stay, and the better ones have qualities that are well suited to the kind of writing and circumstances of writing that face our students today. A good quality fountain pen, with satisfactory ink flow, a nib suited to the individual's writing, and a barrel that fits his or her hand comfortably might be best for some children, but not all. Wherever possible I believe in having a free choice of writing implements. It would be a help if teachers were flexible enough to allow children to experiment with various kinds of pens to find out what suits them and their handwriting. Simple pen preference tests are interesting for all concerned, and are the best way of finding out what best suits your particular group of children.

I have nothing against fountain pens except when they are imposed on left-handers, adding to their difficulties, and resulting in smudged work. I only wish that they were the quality product that they once were. Nowadays it is seldom possible to test a pen before purchasing it to try out the nib, and it is the nib that is most important to the writer. Then there is the matter of the ink flow. Cartridge pens vary considerably, and price is not always an accurate guide to how well they will perform. But there is more to it than that. If any adults need reminding that personal choice of pen point, barrel size or shape, length or even material is individual then I suggest that at any gathering, all those present are asked to change pens with their neighbours. They will soon experience the reason for the exercise. What one person finds best to write with, the next one heartily dislikes. If we want our pupils to write freely and comfortably, then some of the dictatorial regulations that have long outlived their use, must be relaxed.

The real answer seems to be that different pens require different penholds. There is a very efficient alternative penhold that works better with modern pens, and is probably more relaxed and certainly less likely to be painful, than the traditional tripod grip when used under pressure for long periods of writing such as at examination time. It is easier to illustrate it than to describe. Do try it, you may not like it yourself, but it may be the best thing for some of your tense or awkward pupils.

*The alternative penhold*

If pupils are able to write fast enough to keep up, without pain and without distorting the letterforms, then, however awkward their penhold may look to you it may be best to leave the situation alone. Unless you can provide a good enough reason to motivate them to alter, then you are unlikely to succeed, and quite likely their solution suits them better than yours. The best that you can do is to explain that if that penhold should begin to slow them down as the demand for speed increases, or if it begins to cause them discomfort, then they should experiment themselves to find something better. Many twisted penholds have arisen because of inappropriate paper position, so the paper will need to go further to the side of the writing hand, and may need to be slanted too, before the penhold can be altered.

## ■ A balanced view of joining

Why is it that so many views on handwriting issues are extreme and unbalanced? When it comes to the matter of joins I have to tell many children that their handwriting problems are caused by the fact that they are joining up too much. It is easy to demonstrate to them the advantages of penlifts so that their hand can move comfortably along the line as they write, producing relaxed letters and joins. Many of these unfortunate children tell me that if they were to do this at school they would be 'told off' for not joining every letter all the time. Sometimes they are so desperate that they take a penlift and then disguise it with a false joining stroke afterwards. Yet joins are meant to facilitate fast efficient mature handwriting. They are not meant as an instrument of torture. Children need to learn how all the letters join, and then to use them as appropriate. Joining letters is not a complex matter, and I often wonder why it becomes such an emotive issue. All that is necessary, when children can produce basic separate letters with the correct movement, is to keep the pencil on the paper when moving from the end of one letter to the beginning of the next. The National Curriculum document recognises this when it encourages early joins, rather than the retention of neat separate letters until the age of seven or beyond. If your pupils are not joining up when they reach your schools, then after you have checked their letters for movement faults, explain how simple it all is and encourage them to join. You can start with the simplest joins first: those that join from the baseline.

Joining will be most difficult for those who pride themselves on their neat print script. That is why I recommend that all infants are taught letters that have integral exit strokes from the start. The abrupt letters of print script result in real difficulties. They mean that children have to take the pressure off the terminal of the letter at the baseline, and change direction at the same time, before the letters can flow and join. Letters with exits promote a more relaxed hand position, movement and pressure, all of which lead to spontaneous joins along the baseline. It is undeniable that children's first attempts at joined up cannot be as neat as their separate letters, and such children find it difficult to relax their self-set standard. It is up to the teacher to explain the advantages of joins, and to have a balanced attitude to the level of joining. Roughly speaking, round letters join less easily than oval slanting ones, which permit very simple ligatures to letters such as a, d, c, g, o and q. This does not mean that all children should or could be made to write oval slanting letters. On the whole, large writing needs more rests than small writing, and left-handers may need more penlifts than right-handers, but it is not a matter of an exact count of how many letters before a penlift, nor precisely which letters should join and which should not. The complexity of the strokes within the letters and their position within the word often influence the frequency of penlifts.

Most adults lift their pen from the paper every few letters. Why, therefore, do they insist that children should not be allowed to do likewise. We are not living in the last century when quills were used and it was inadvisable to stop in the middle of a word in case the pen spluttered ink all over the page. In those days writers were carefully trained not to rest the whole hand on the table while writing, but to balance lightly on their little finger. This allowed the pen to glide easily along the line, but it is not easy, and certainly is not a realistic way of dealing with modern pens.

Instruction is meant to give pupils efficient handwriting that works as effortlessly as possible for them. If it is beautiful then that is an added benefit, but as long as it is legible and preferably consistent, as well as being capable of being speeded up to the almost impossible speed needed for note-taking and passing examinations, then you, the teacher, need not be too worried. Children do not willingly write badly. Many of the pupils who face daily criticism of their writing (joined or not) are so tense and unhappy about it that this in itself is enough to distort letters and invite even further loss of marks and derogatory remarks at the bottom of their work. If something is really wrong with their handwriting then pupils need informed diagnosis and help, otherwise try a bit of praise instead of criticism, it often works wonderfully well.

## ■ Understanding left-handedness

Left-handers deserve special mention. Some never have any problems with writing, drawing or any other precision tasks, but others have considerable difficulties with a writing system that undoubtedly works better for right-handers. Some, but not all such problems, need not have occurred at all if sufficient thought had been given to left-handers' needs in the infant school. Left-handers need practical help from the start to develop strategies to deal with their special requirements. The most important and often neglected advice concerns paper position. If left-handers are taught to place their paper to their left side many difficulties can be avoided. This allows them to see what they are doing, or have written, without bending their bodies sideways or twisting their wrists over the top of the line of writing. It also helps to avoid smudged work. If the paper is to go to the left side, then there must be enough space, and when left-handers sit next to their right-handed friends, then it should be to the side where they do not jog each other as they write. Classrooms are often organised for right-handers, so it is necessary to ensure that left-handers have enough light to see what they are doing. In the early stages children need softish

pencils that do not dig into the paper, not hard sharp points. Modern fibre-tipped pens are ideal for left-handers. They move easily and do not smudge. All these practical points are quite simple to organise, but can make considerable differences in children's ability to write and to their whole attitude to written tasks.

Many left-handers have writing that slopes backwards. This should not matter unless the slant is excessive and affects the legibility of the writing. Some teachers find a backwards slanting writing somehow reprehensible, and criticise children without realising that slant is a result of how the pen is manipulated. A forward slant can be difficult for young left-handers. The easiest way to produce a forward slant is for the child to twist (invert) the wrist. This then invites more criticism. I am not alone in suggesting that there might be slightly backward slanting models for those who otherwise are always striving to attain the (almost) impossible. Certain letters are particularly difficult for left-handers. The worst are f and s because they involve a change of direction. Children can be helped to simplify these letters and to find the form that is easiest for them to write. Working together to design personal letters is a particularly satisfying exercise, bridging the 'them and us' situation that often arises in handwriting criticism.

If any of you who normally use your right hands, had to spend a day or so using only your left hands then it might be easier to understand what it feels like to be in that position permanently. In countries where the curriculum sets specific guidelines for dealing with left-handers fewer problems are reported. This leads me to the conclusion that many left-handers who fail to achieve their optimum are victims of an unsympathetic system.

There are more serious problems, too. These are concerned with directionality, a little understood aspect of our physical make up. A left-hander usually draws a line more easily from right to left, so, for example, t and f will be crossed in that direction. This may prevent left-handers from using some of the shortcuts available to right-handers but it is no real problem. The trouble arises when the right-to-left directional pull is so strong that the writer finds difficulty in proceeding in the correct direction within separate letters or between them, and occasionally within whole words. Young children may persist in starting at the wrong place and writing in the wrong direction, resulting in mirror writing. Later on joining is difficult. Left-handers' difficulties may be disguised as slow at copying down, or just untidy, and their problems can only be understood by observing them in the act of writing. One unfortunate left-hander described how he could neither control nor understand his urge to go right round a letter and backwards. This always happened when he tried to write neatly and slowly to please his teacher. If he wrote fast the momentum seemed to carry him in the right direction, but then he was criticised for untidy writing. If you have such a child in your class make use of him or her. Ask the child to explain the way he or she feels, and how strong the urge is to go in the 'wrong' direction. This is the best way to learn how to help such problems. Some children can be helped to develop techniques to overcome this directional pull, but occasionally it is so strong that all exercises fail and a word processor may be the answer. By that time the pupil may scan and even spell from right to left, a problem to which I still have no answer.

There are a few cases where the wrong decision concerning a preferred hand has been made for a young child. This may not become evident until many years later. All concerned have to be very sure before changing, as the writer will take some time before becoming practised and fast enough with the other hand. In such cases the paper position will also have to be altered and re-automated, and some letterforms may have to be modified.

## ■ Handwriting is an indicator

Handwriting is not just a simple matter of letters, neat or untidy. It is a physical act that involves not only the hand but the whole body. It interacts with other cognitive tasks, and above all is affected by, and in turn reflects, the writer's emotions and attitudes. This makes handwriting an ideal diagnostic tool. You as their teacher are in an ideal position to chart the ups and downs of your pupils through their handwriting. I see children only once, but glancing through their books it is not difficult to see which subjects are boring or perhaps stressful. It is all too easy to see where tensions are building up, and handwriting deteriorating as a result. The date may suggest that some very important examinations are near, but the tension may just as easily indicate the breakup of their parents' marriage, a bereavement or a bout of bullying. All that I know is that the tension is an indicator, and a little gentle questioning may discover the cause; then an explanation may defuse a difficult situation. You may know the reason, but may be unable to do much about it, other than offering sympathy. However, by recognising the cause of the tense writing rather than criticising the distorted result, an injustice is avoided. An unhappy child will not be able to avoid the uneven or jagged strokes that he or she cannot control, just as poor spellers cannot achieve fluent writing as long as they are uncertain of which letter should come next. An intelligent child with an awkward body may never achieve the smooth writing that comes easily to others, however hard he (it is more often boys who suffer this way) may try to please. Never ignore complaints of persistent headaches, backaches or other pain. They are important indicators of problems that may need medical attention.

## Vision and pain

Both vision and pain concern the body. It is surprising how often the eyes are at fault when learning difficulties are present. Faults are not usually of the obvious long- or short-sighted type that are easily checked by the school nurse, although in several cases such a minor condition has been found to be the cause in those misdiagnosed as dyslexics, dyspraxics or some other umbrella classification. When pupils are engrossed in their school work it is often quite easy to spot those with obscure visual problems. Look for those who hold their heads at an awkward angle, those who keep losing their place, those with uneven margins or word spacing. If you watch their eye movements you can get more of an idea of what is wrong. There are plenty of reasons why children might be good at oral work and poor at written exercises, but those with the most usual difficulty, no leading eye, have specific problems with the central area of a page, where they are likely to change from using one eye to the other. These children will not be happy on the computer, and they may have trouble adding columns of figures. Other children (if asked) find difficulty in seeing the board from some angles. I am not expecting you to turn into eye specialists overnight, only to become aware of some of the conditions that come within the speciality of orthoptics. A G.P. referral is all that is needed. A visit to an orthoptist or informed optometrist is seldom a waste of time, and can provide amazing results for those for whom their remediation was necessary. The responses that echo in my mind are from those children whose lives have been blighted because such simple tests have been left until their teenage years, 'if only this had been discovered before how different my life would have been'.

Maybe it seems a lot to ask of a busy teacher to be aware of so many matters, but it does not take much to ask every now and then if everyone can see clearly, hear distinctly, and one more question: does anyone suffer discomfort or even pain when writing? This is the first question that I pose when confronted with a group of older pupils, and I am often horrified by the proportion who reply in the affirmative. It is not always so prevalent in younger ones whose pliant bodies can put up with quite a lot of distortion before they experience actual pain. I remember asking a class of twenty-nine ten year old boys and their teacher how many of them experienced pain. Twenty-eight of the boys, plus the teacher put up their hand. The teacher then came out with the extraordinary statement that of course handwriting was painful, it was a discipline. This is precisely the attitude that I want to dispute. Pain is the body's warning system, it should not be ignored, or you risk developing that disturbing condition called writer's cramp when the body refuses to obey instructions to wield a pen or pencil, but will perform any other precision task.

Pain seems to be the result of poor writing posture or strategies exacerbated when the demands for speed, and tension from other causes combine. Do warn your pupils that pain or discomfort should not be ignored and that they should feel free to complain about the furniture if that is the cause. Pupils should then experiment with paper positions or penholds that allow their bodies to write (or read) in a more relaxed position.

It is sensible, but sadly rather futile, to understand that a slanting surface is far easier to write on or read from. The comfortable old-fashioned desks have almost all been scrapped in the interests of 'efficiency' in the modern classroom. All that can be said is that if a child has a tremor for any reason, a slant will be of real assistance, and in such cases it is quite easy to test for the best angle, and make one up in the carpentry class. If any other pupils feel that they would prefer to have a slanting work surface, an atlas propped on a couple of books, or even their ever-present looseleaf file with the fatter end further from their body, can provide a comfortable slant without attracting too much attention. Such assistance costs little or nothing, and can make a real difference to pupils' performance as well as their attitudes to their work.

None of these circumstances are an excuse for poor handwriting. They are just a recognition of the realities of the task. Allowances are not likely to be made in the harsh atmosphere of the outside world, and pupils have to realise that they may be judged by their handwriting even before people meet them. However, employers and others are influenced by many factors other than conventional neatness. Strength of character, originality and maturity may be equally important in many circumstances, and all these characteristics leave their mark for the experienced observer to interpret. For schoolchildren it should be enough to expect them to perform to their optimum rather than to some arbitrary norm, and for their teachers to be able to see when outside factors are causing excessive tension, to refrain from criticism in such circumstances and to try to uncover and remedy the cause. Handwriting need not be a series of problems. For the majority of pupils (if the vital first two years of teaching has been successful) the lightest of touches is needed. This enables handwriting to mature as the pupils themselves develop.

# ■ Presentation

Marks in examinations are supposedly allotted for the general appearance and presentation of work, yet what does this word presentation mean? If you ask several schools what they mean by the word presentation, and what their policy for teaching or judging it is, you will get varying replies. Some people will shelter behind the word neatness. But neat handwriting alone will not necessarily provide a page that is easy to read. In reality, some over-neat handwriting is extremely difficult to decipher. Other schools have strict rules about such matters as margins or the underlining of titles. That will not solve the problem either.

When I put this proposition to the head of a local primary school, well-known for the excellent presentation of all its work in the widest sense, the answer that he gave me was far from simple. He felt that pride in work, and therefore good presentation comes from a supportive atmosphere throughout the whole school.

Presentation then, is a much wider issue than just written work. Tidiness, from the school office down to how the children are encouraged to keep their desks in order needs considering. The way school buildings and grounds are kept up contributes, too. Not everyone is artistic and the concept of a well laid out page is not a common skill, so whoever has that skill should be used in an advisory position. The newest teacher may have a better perception of layout than a much more experienced member of staff and some children may have a better concept of layout than some teachers.

This particular head had the idea that instilling good mounting skills was a definite aid to instilling pride in individual's work from an early age. He admitted that in his school, presentation had received high priority during the time of the two previous heads, and there had been continuity of staff that had also helped matters. He felt that getting young children involved in the mounting of their work involved them in qualitative judgements and visual discrimination. This is certainly good practice. It is just these skills that are lacking in so many children's experience today. He combined written and painted techniques, sometimes attending painting sessions himself to join in with the activities. The children are encouraged to use coloured paper, not always white, and to write with anything appropriate. He suggested bringing in, from the start, parallels between art and writing. By using what he calls visual interruption in the written work on every page, he was instilling the rudiments of presentation that would aid the reader, as well as making the page look more attractive. The techniques used cut-outs, and often a colour focus to divide up text into logical chunks.

This head said that good presentation as an example to children (as well as any visitor to the school) started at the gate with a well-presented notice-board. The school tries to make sure that everything that the children see is well presented, right down to the teachers' handwriting in pupils' exercise books. Corrections are dealt with in a manner that does not result in plastering the page with red ink. Pencil is used to point out errors but not so that it spoils the appearance of the work.

Recognising that such a system needs time to become effective, he encourages discussion of presentation skills throughout the school. New teachers are introduced to the concepts, and everyone is invited to comment on any ideas on show, and are encouraged to copy the successful ones in an atmosphere that does not involve a sense of cribbing. Above all he stressed the need to start early, if the whole idea of good presentation is to carry through into later school life.

I can report on the success of this school's policy. When involved with teenagers' handwriting in local secondary schools, teachers reported that they could always tell which pupils had attended this school, because of the layout and appearance of their exercise books, though it had to be admitted, this praise did not always extend to the legibility of the pupils' handwriting.

It is certainly easier to instill good layout skills in the junior school where the sheets of paper are usually smaller than the obligatory A4 sheets that are used in secondary school. A few more ideas on layout are expressed on page 17 at the end of the section entitled 'Specially for secondary schools'.

## The lessons to be learned

What are the lessons that can be learned from this rather special school's policy regarding presentation?

1 That an awareness of presentation can and should be instilled from the start.
2 That respect for children's work, and their attitudes to their own work are both involved.
3 That presentation is a matter of considering the reader, and the way that a reader might best assimilate any particular text, as much as the neatness of handwriting.
4 That presentation does not have to consist of a strict list of rules.

## Page layout

What does contribute to a well laid out page?

1 Good margins, at both sides of the page.
2 Good spacing under headings and between sections.
3 Consistency of handwriting in terms of slant and proportion of letters and word spacing, rather than any particular style of handwriting.

These all contribute to neatness in the sense that they allow the eye to travel easily over the text. Good spacing and organisation of text assists assimilation and appreciation of a piece of writing at any age or stage.

Poor spelling and too many rubbings out invite criticism of untidiness. The tensions resulting from such a problem will make writing look more uneven and jagged, and even poorly spaced as the pressures of writing are reflected in the uneven pressure of the pen on the paper. Unrealistically slow, neat handwriting may invite praise, but instill in the writer the idea that only slow handwriting is worth anything – an inhibiting habit for a high achiever who needs speed. Even the letters written by children who may suffer from a condition causing a considerable tremor can be improved with good spacing and layout. These examples alone try to balance attitudes to so-called neatness. In all eventualities, neatness is a subjective matter, with some people liking one kind of neatness, while it offends another.

## Rules

Some of the rules of presentation that I have been shown in school policies are the antithesis of good presentation as I understand it. The obsession with underlining titles can be ugly in the extreme if used with certain types of writing or if the line is too close under almost any handwriting. The requirement to use capital letters for titles usually misfires too. Capital letters are seldom as well formed as small letters. Few people have a level of capital letters that would embellish a title and improve a page. In recent years I have been involved in judging a national handwriting competition, where it is to be expected that presentation would play a large part in the planning as well as the marking of entries. It has frequently been noticeable that even teachers' entries have been spoiled by the use of underlined capital letters in headings. Some children, who appear to have defied their teachers, leave good spaces underneath a heading that has been written in their ordinary handwriting. This is usually effective, standing out in a pile of entries which have followed the perceived rules. This again demonstrates how some children possess innate layout skills. They are lucky, rather than clever. Such skills are rare in both adults and children.

Margins often seem to be an obsession with those who like to dictate rules. Some schools state definitely that margins are permitted only on the left side. Anything else is a waste of paper. Along with that come instructions that lines should not be left between sections, and never between paragraphs. Yet some handwriting cries out for such spaces. Small, dense writing needs space for the eye to rest; and large, open writing has the same requirement, though for a different reason. Such matters cannot be confined to a narrow set of rules.

The way forward should involve more discussion and comparison and much less criticism. If teachers themselves are not sure what constitutes this difficult issue of how spacing relates to the size and weight of letters, and to the length of a text, then a selection of pupils' work would best provide clues to what is achievable with the tools and conditions within your school. You may find that some children possess this innate sense of good layout that it is so difficult to define, much less to teach.

# ■ Specially for secondary schools

Many children leave primary school with handwriting that is not adequate to cope with the new demands of secondary school life. Under pressure of speed, with note-taking and the general raised expectation for all written work, their handwriting will break down. Of course a proportion will have had a good enough start to enable them to develop a fast, efficient hand, but many pupils need help, and the sooner they get it the better.

Handwriting is such a personal matter that by eleven or twelve it is too late to suggest imposing a general model on a whole school, and the idea that there are a few magic exercises or a simple formula to cure all problems, is to underestimate the difficulties and insult both teacher and pupil.

So what can be done when criticism of their handwriting too often sends pupils scurrying back to the safety of print or results in an even tenser cursive? What each pupil really needs is a careful diagnosis of the problem which has developed, and individual, sympathetic help in working out a solution. This diagnosis does not take long once you have learned the techniques involved.

# ■ Three approaches to handwriting problems

In many schools a one-to-one approach may not always be practical, so this book suggests three approaches to tackling handwriting problems; they are not mutually exclusive:

1 That you make a quick assessment, in random groups of five or six, during the first term. This enables you to pick out those with the worst problems, to promote an interest in efficient handwriting and explain the changing demands of the new school life.
2 That you pick out those whose handwriting is in most need of help, irrespective of their academic attainment, or age, and give them individual help.
3 That as a whole-form or tutor-group activity, irrespective of the year, you discuss handwriting positively, putting forward suggestions as to how pupils can help themselves to more efficient, legible handwriting. In this way you soon pick out the few with serious problems and encourage those with less obvious difficulties to experiment and improve.

Section 3 can be used with any of these approaches. It enables handwriting problems to be tackled sympathetically by any member of staff and need not be confined to the remedial department. Science, History or Language specialists are just as appropriate as English or Art teachers; and P.E. instructors may well be best qualified to spot and deal with posture and grip problems.

## Using the three approaches

1 The test sentences on page 28 can be set to small groups and analysed later. The teacher may wish to spend the duration of the testing time observing the pupils and making notes of *how* each one writes (grip, posture, paper position etc.). This allows individual diagnosis and the pupil can then be given that part of section 3 which will be of most help.
2 Any teacher, having learned the diagnostic techniques explained on pages 20–28 should quickly get to the root of a pupil's individual problems and be able to help guide them through the checklists, and perhaps set up a voluntary lunchtime self-help club for those with handwriting problems.
3 Any part of section 3 can be used for class discussion, or be set as homework. Short essays on some of the points raised on page 30 can help pupils to become aware of some of the problems, of both the writer and the reader, and to find solutions for themselves. If tackled, in this way handwriting can be made an interesting topic, not a chore.

Each of the three suggested approaches has its advantages and serves slightly different needs. Undoubtedly pupils with deep-seated problems will need really informed individual diagnosis and constructive back-up for some time. Problems do not just go away; they become more difficult to diagnose and to cure the longer they are left.

An early survey (perhaps during the first few weeks of the new school year) will ensure that those in most need get help as soon as possible. However, no school will want to assume overall direction of handwriting; it is too personal a matter and too much formal emphasis can be counter-productive as it is often interpreted as urging neatness and good presentation only. It is this that makes insecure pupils revert to print. The emphasis should always be on a legible but fast and efficient way of writing.

This is where the third approach comes into its own. For some pupils an accurate awareness of a problem will be enough. Such individuals will be able to use the relevant parts of section 3 to spot their own faults and by experimenting with either the practical suggestions, or the movement exercises, more or less cure themselves. This is teaching the very quality needed, self-criticism. The sooner the cure is put into the hands of the pupils themselves, the better. Older pupils certainly respond well to this reasoned approach. The confidence gained from self-motivation and self-help is soon reflected in their written work and promotes all round improvement. Encouragement is needed and not too much coercion.

# ■ Presentation and layout in the secondary school

The issues involved in presentation now shift slightly. Whereas the priority in junior schools might be to instil a concept of pride in work, and an ability to lift the level of presentation when work is to be put on show, in secondary schools the issue is more about how to make longer passages of text easier for the reader to assimilate.

It is not an easy task to try to analyse the reasons why teachers sometimes write comments on older pupils' work such as 'poorly presented', 'untidy' or 'illegible'. Ask a group of teachers what their concept of illegibility or poor presentation is and you will get a surprising variety of answers:

1 Poor handwriting.
2 Erasures or frequent spelling corrections.
3 Irregular or inadequate margins often allied to small or variable sized handwriting.
4 Wide or irregular word spacing often allied to large margins, which may be seen as wasteful.
5 Non-standard titling conventions, e.g. underlining, capitals, etc., which can invite criticism even though the pupils' conventions may suit the writing better than the schools'.

To lay out a page of lined A4 paper is not easy, even for a skilled adult. Leaving aside the handwriting aspect of presentation, I hope that the contents of this book will have led to a greater understanding of the causes of handwriting problems, and the need to relax tensions. Confident, consistent personal handwriting is certainly a positive step towards good presentation.

Confidence is needed in presentation, but other issues are involved as well. The first and most important is an ability to organise text. Going back a stage further, the writer needs to have a clear idea of how to plan the essay, or piece of writing. That means where and how to insert subtitles and spaces to divide up the page. Of course such planning strategies go hand in hand with planning the contents of written work.

All this is theoretical. How can the classroom teacher get these ideas over? Handwritten text is difficult and time consuming to handle when experimenting with different layouts. The computer, however, manipulates chunks of text very easily. In addition any daily newspaper provides examples of the hierarchies of titles and subtitles. Make use of both these facilities to demonstrate different page layouts and conventions. Then combine presentation of work with strategies for the organisation of text not only to benefit visual appearance but to improve compositional strategies.

# ■ A final warning

Just a word of warning; the schemes in this book will, initially, work in the opposite direction from that which pupils ultimately need. This analytical, self-critical approach should be seen as a temporary, short-term measure for training or retraining. It can make people too aware of their writing as a technique, whereas handwriting, like so many other skills, only becomes really efficient when performed automatically. The mind needs to be free to concentrate on the content of written work without worrying about the action of writing and there is a fine balance between persuading those with difficulties to concentrate on individual letters while they are retraining, whilst maintaining awareness of their long term objectives.

To be relevant to all pupils this book has to appeal to, and cover, a wide age and ability range. It assumes, without minimising the problems, a basic level of achievement. Teachers will, however, sometimes be faced with pupils whose writing falls far below this level. A thorough programme of instruction must be applied in such cases, starting from whatever point is appropriate. The principles of such a programme should be identical to those already described but should be applied by means of simpler exercises and greater supervision.

**Some remedial exercises from sections 2 and 3**

ililil ininin hnhnhn

mumu nmhr nhuy

ill hill in my mum

hit hunt minimum

oooooo ovovovov

owowow ororororo

row vow own room

word wool horror

fa fi fo fu fat flit

ta ti to tu tip lift

the thin with other

kitty fitting off off

acaca adada agaga

cecece dedede aqaq

no do go dad laced

added caged jagged

# 2
# Diagnosis and remediation

# ■ Starting out

Let us start by assuming that you are seeing a pupil for the first time. You may already be familiar with his or her problems but this method will help you to look at long-standing worries with a fresh outlook and ensure that you will be able to tackle any newcomer's difficulties.

Something that the pupil has already written will help you to make general judgements. It will show up inconsistencies in size, slant or spacing. It can give you a fair idea of how tense the writer is. You may be able to detect incorrectly formed letters this way, but it is seldom enough to enable you to make an accurate diagnosis.

You *must* see the writer in action. This is the only way to judge whether the poor writing is caused by bad physical habits, an incorrect writing movement or a combination of both.

Diagnosis can be divided into three stages:
1 Observation.
2 Procedure.
3 Assessment.

# ■ Stage 1: observation

## Posture problems

First observe *how* the pupil has been writing. This is just as relevant as, and has of course influenced, *what* has been written.

Let the pupils sit and write a few familiar words, perhaps their name and school. While they are doing this you have a chance to spot faults in writing posture. This term 'writing posture' is not confined to sitting up straight; it includes how pupils hold their pens, and what their wrists, arms, necks and shoulders are doing; it is dependent on the position of the writer's paper and often on the height of the chair or desk.

See pages 30–39 of section 3 where pen hold, paper position and other practical aspects of handwriting are explained.

You need to observe:

1 Whether the standard chair is either too high or too low for the writer. Tall children may be unable to get their knees under small school desks. Sitting sideways can become habitual and continue long after the cause has been removed. Short children have more obvious problems but these too can have long-lasting effects on their writing posture.
2 Whether the pupil is able to sit straight with no undue tension to neck or shoulders. You can judge this more easily from behind the chair.
3 Where the paper is positioned in relation to the mid-line of the body. This must be related to right or left-handedness. Notice the angle of the paper.

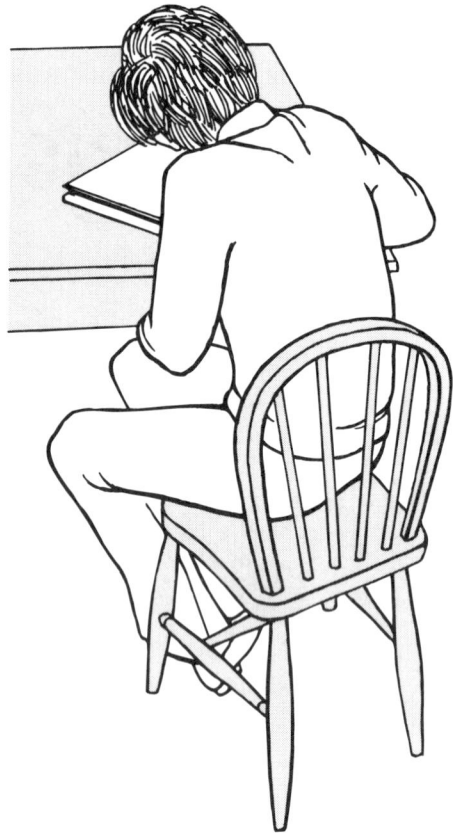

*The furniture must fit the pupil. Too high or, as in this case, too low a chair prevents the writer from sitting properly. The relationship of chair to desk height is as important as chair to leg length.*

4 How the arm is held; whether it is clamped close to the body, has to stretch across the body or is able to move freely from the shoulder.
5 How the wrist is positioned; inverted or non-inverted. The angle of the wrist may determine whether the pen comes from above, the side or below the line of writing.
6 The hand position; whether it is on edge, slightly flattened or perhaps excessively so. If it is too much on edge you should already have picked this up, as this usually entails a twist of the wrist.
7 The finger position; how many fingers are on the pen and whether the thumb or one of the fingers is nearest to the pen point. Notice the angle of the forefinger. The importance of all this is explained in section 3.

## Letter problems

Please read pages 43–63 in section 3 where the letter faults are explained quite clearly.

You need to become so aware of the movement of letters that you can immediately spot wrongly-formed letters, while a pupil is writing or in a written sample.

As a quick guide to the commonest faults check:

1 Point of entry and direction of stroke.
2 Strokes that are missing from letters.
3 Letters that are the wrong height.

The next step is to note how much the letters are joined and how well they are joined. Check the joins, group by group, bearing in mind that 'bad' writing is often caused by poor joins.

You should then judge how consistent the other elements of handwriting are: size, slant, alignment, letter and word spacing must all be taken into account.

Notice if there is any evidence of tremor, or significant differences in line quality. These may signal a slight handicap or be a sign of tension.

## Tension

Tension shows up in so many ways, and has many different causes. It can distort handwriting to such an extent that it can mask the true state of affairs. You must note whether the pen is gripped excessively hard or is pressed over hard into the paper. These are the easiest signs of physical tension to spot.

You must watch to see if there is undue hesitation or changes of pressure during long or unfamiliar words. This signals, among other things, that the problem may lie in tension induced by poor spelling. (Tension caused by other learning difficulties can show in handwriting. This confuses the issue because it suggests that the writing is at fault when there is nothing basically wrong with it.

Uneven spacing and unexplained differences in letter size or slant can also signal extreme tension. Strokes or even complete letters can be left out. You must take great care to get the pupil relaxed before attempting a diagnosis. First of all, without the stress

there may be little wrong with the actual writing.More important still, any criticism will result in more tension and further deterioration

You may wonder why there is no reference to neatness or presentation. This would provide too general a judgement at this stage. Writing will get tidier as the faults get untangled and dealt with. Keep those untidy samples for comparison later on, but deal with specific issues first.

## Speed

Speed is complex because so many issues are involved. How can you judge accurately whether a child's hesitation is caused by tension, poor spelling, lack of concentration, or the act of writing? The usual test asks a child or a whole group to repeat a phrase over and over again for several minutes. Letters are counted, averages are taken but what has been proved? Such a test will favour the ambitious pupil who will enjoy the race against the clock no matter what it does to the standard of writing. You may misjudge the more honest pupils who know what speed is best for their writing, and upset the ones with real problems. This is not going to help you much with your diagnosis.

Look at speed in a different way. Absolute speed says nothing about the speed at which a particular pupil ought to write. Each person has an optimum speed to think and to make slow thinkers speed up causes nothing but confusion. The same applies to handwriting. If the optimum speed is exceeded the writing will fall apart. There is only a problem if the pupil's optimum speed is not being reached.

Perhaps in the early stage of assessment, only two simple questions are necessary.

1 Can you write as fast as you want to?
2 Do you feel you could write legibly any faster than you do?

*A typical example of tension and unhappiness showing through handwriting. This intelligent 14-year-old has problems that are not concerned with actual letterforms. He needs understanding and encouragement, not criticism.*

# Stage 2: procedure

Relaxation, confidence and motivation are all needed. In a few cases this is all that is necessary! Those pupils who have been criticised for having a personal style different from the school model, or one that offends their parents will quickly warm to sympathetic assurance. The tenseness and uneven look to their writing should soon disappear. With confidence, small, cramped writing should start to flow. To give this kind of assurance you must of course have made quite sure that there are no basic faults in the writing movement.

The first session is most important. You have made your initial observations; how should you proceed in a one to one situation?

1 Provide a good selection of pens for the pupils to try. Offer lined and unlined paper. If you give a choice then you will set the right atmosphere. Show from the start that you are on the pupils' side.
2 You can do without words or even letters in the first exercises. This takes the pressure off those with multiple learning difficulties. It also makes your job easier.

Let the pupil try the relaxing exercises on page 42 of section 3. Read the page together or, if you prefer, you can do the explaining.

You can learn a great deal from these scribbles when you know how to interpret them. They show up hesitation, excess pressure or difficulty in producing a particular stroke. You will have to decide the exact cause but you now have a visible trace of any practical faults the pupil may have. This sample is valuable; keep it carefully so both of you can *see* the progress as you tackle the problems. The next step is to deal with any postural faults.

## Procedure for dealing with posture

1 Make sure the chair is a comfortable height; if not get a cushion, move to another desk or do whatever is necessary to ensure that the writer sits up properly. I am assuming that you have arranged for good lighting for either right or left hander. If the writing surface is poor, provide a pad. Each stage in changing bad conditions, and also showing that you care, can show improvement in the written trace. Repeat the scribble exercise and observe and discuss any differences.
2 Paper position is also important. Remember that all these practical factors are interdependent; change one and they all alter. Where you place your paper is vital because it often determines whether you can see what you are doing. Writers may need to move the paper to left or right or experiment with a different slant. Then they will be able to sit up properly, straighten the waist or allow their arm to move more freely or correct whatever has been wrong. This simple alteration usually makes a great difference. However, it does bring into play new and unaccustomed muscles so some pupils may resist the change at first. If an explanation is not enough to convince the pupil do not insist. It is vital to gain confidence in this first session. You must score a success somehow, so switch to a letter fault that you are more confident of solving. You can always return to penhold or paper position at the next session.
3 Penhold is a complex business. Try to forget preconceived ideas and judge each case on its merits. Consult section 3 and read the pages on both conventional and unconventional holds carefully. It is not sufficient to ask whether the penhold is conventional or not. 'Does it work for you?' is a more relevant question. If a penhold is causing pain, stopping a pupil from writing fast enough or unduly distorting letters, then something must be done.

Pain is the easiest to deal with because the benefit is obvious. Your job is to assess which element of the grip is causing the trouble; the fingers, the hand or perhaps the wrist. The principles are explained in section 3, but neither hands nor holds conform to strict rules. You will have to work out any changes together. Remember that the writer has to *want* to change. Without motivation you cannot alter bad habits.

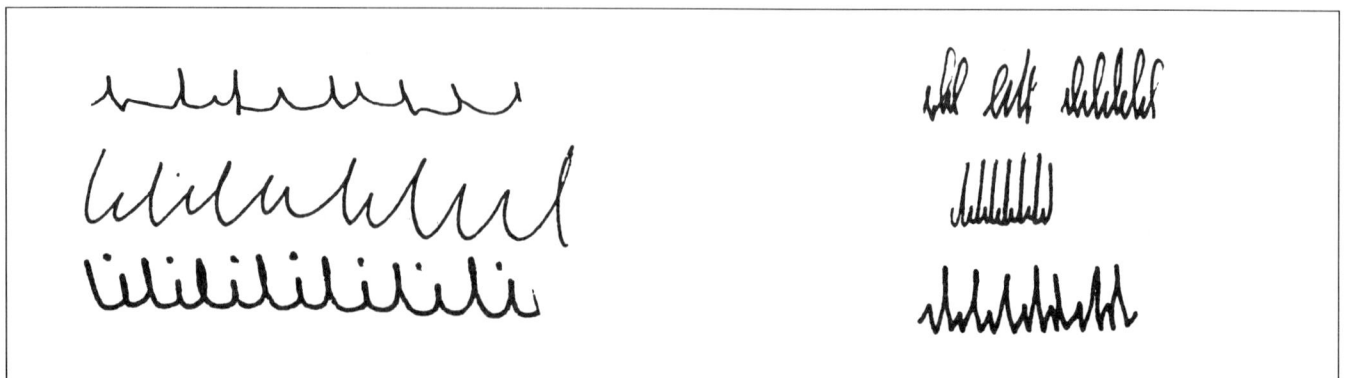

*You can tell a great deal from the simplest patterns. These examples show varying degrees of tension and control. Already you have a fair idea of where each pupil's problems lie.*

Pupils with a problem should alter each element of penhold in turn to see what helps them. You can discuss any changes to their writing but they must decide what feels best. Any alteration, however beneficial, may feel strange at first. You should leave the complex movements that arise in ordinary sentences until the hand gets used to the changes. Start with the relaxing exercises then go on to simple letter patterns. Giving the writer the techniques to work out a personal solution is the best way of reaching a permanent cure.

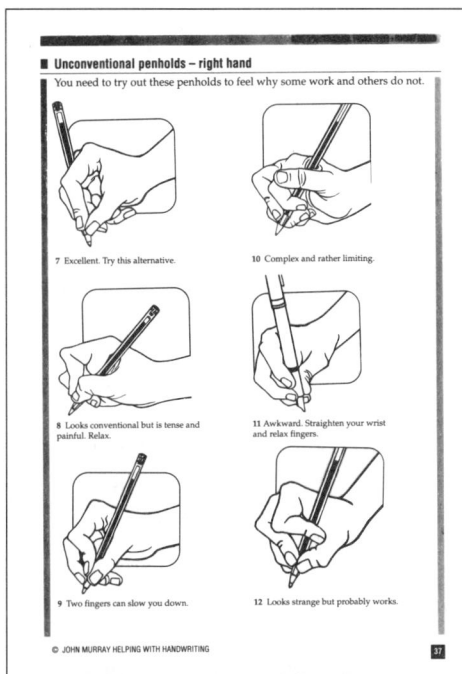

**■ Unconventional penholds – right hand**
You need to try out these penholds to feel why some work and others do not.

7 Excellent. Try this alternative.

10 Complex and rather limiting.

8 Looks conventional but is tense and painful. Relax.

11 Awkward. Straighten your wrist and relax fingers.

9 Two fingers can slow you down.

12 Looks strange but probably works.

© JOHN MURRAY HELPING WITH HANDWRITING

37

Above is a reduced version of some of the unconventional penholds shown in section 3, page 37. More information on this complex subject is given there. These drawings are all taken from actual photographs. They are a sample of those you may find in any group of schoolchildren. With the exception of number 7, they are not meant as teaching models. They can help you decide which penholds to change and which to leave alone. But first you must understand why these penholds have arisen and how each is likely to affect the writer.

Left-handers, allowed to find their own solution, often clear their line of vision by manipulating their hand rather than changing their paper position. This partly accounts for the twisted wrist and perhaps the thumbs tucked out of the way. You will have to alter the paper position before you can do anything about the penholds. The illustrations on page 41 highlight another point that is less easy to understand.

Notice on page 36 how the left-handers have used different strategies to achieve the same pen slant as a right-hander. Hands 1 and 2 have twisted the wrist so the pen comes from above the line of the writing. The top one is worst, try to change this.

Hands 3 and 4 come in from the side. The top one pushes with the thumb and the bottom one tucks the

thumb in. Neither is desirable, but the bottom one is by far the worst.

Hands 5 and 6 come from below the line of writing like most right-handers. The upright pen position is achieved by taking the thumb out of action. Some of this uprightness may be needed to make ballpoints work properly. Bear this in mind as you advise students.

The length of fingers can influence penholds. Long fingers can be cramped in a conventional penhold. Hand 7 provides an alternative. Try it. It solves both pain and pen angle.

Young children often use two fingers to steady the pencil. This happens most frequently when five-year-olds are given extra fat pencils to start with. The habit persists. When the two fingers do not synchromise as in hand 9, there can be trouble.

It is hard to see why holds 10 and 12 evolved. An injury to the index finger is always possible.

Do something about hand 11. Right-handers have no excuse to twist their wrist. The only cause is wrongly positioned paper.

Read the comments on these 12 penholds in section 3 on pages 36 and 37 as well as the other pages (34, 35 and 38) on the hand. Try out any unconventional penhold to feel how it works before deciding whether to advise a writer to change. Remember that some people manage to write well with the most unusual penholds, and it may be unwise to alter them.

*Note: A triangular pen grip can help when changing penhold.*

## Procedure for dealing with letters

You are satisfied that you have isolated the letter problem, but you must first accept that it may be difficult for pupils to change their habits. They may have trouble in programming a new movement or they may not even be able to perceive the differences between a correct letter and their own. Your first job will be to explain why the writing fault makes it difficult for anyone else to decipher the words. It may help to trace back to how a habit started. If you can shift some of the 'blame' onto early childhood habits and explain perhaps that it is a common problem with quick writers, you can often defuse a tense situation. You do not have to look far for a logical explanation either, though it is up to you how much you disclose! Bad handwriting is more often the result of bad teaching than any fault on the part of the pupil. You must understand that a child with poor writing will have been subject to constant criticism. If they had received informed help earlier they would not be in their present state. You may be their last chance, and they deserve an honest explanation of their plight. When you have their confidence you have several options:

1 You can find examples of the specific fault in section 3 and use them to explain why the fault

needs to be dealt with. With sensitive pupils it may be better to focus on the sample rather than their own writing.

2 You can use the appropriate sample sentence from page 28 of this section. These sentences are meant to be used in various ways: to reinforce diagnosis, to emphasise the fault to the writer and then to practice to cure it.

*Note: Pupils may well prefer to invent their own sentences.*

3 You can launch straight into correcting the written sample. This is the most direct and, if it succeeds, the quickest method.

## Exercises

The principles of repetitive letter and word exercises are dealt with in great detail in section 3. You will find exercises for most faults there, and will quickly learn how to make up any others that may prove necessary.

*These examples are found on page 45.*

You may find that more mature pupils need only diagnostic help. Provide them with the relevant page, and they can work out their own solutions. Radical alterations are sometimes needed and you may worry that this will slow pupils down. This is of course exactly what will happen because when you concentrate on letter forms, writing ceases to be automatic. You must balance the temporary inconvenience against the benefits of retraining and make sure that the pupil understands and agrees that it is worthwhile.

Be prepared for surprises. The cases that you expect to be the easiest can show up unexpected perceptual or motor problems. You may need considerable ingenuity and have to try a combination of approaches to solve them.

Be generous with praise for the slightest improvement, and do not expect miracles. Some pupils may take a long time before a new movement becomes automatic. Until then, each time the corrected letter occurs the pupil has to make a conscious effort to overcome the habitual movement. This explains why it is possible to do quite well during a remedial session but regress during creative writing tasks. The mind is concentrating on content and lets the hand go on in its accustomed way.

You need to have the co-operation of all the members of staff who deal with the pupils that you are retraining. They can give the extra encouragement that helps so much.

## Group therapy

You may be dealing with groups of pupils either from choice or necessity. Whatever the reason you will find the diagnostic sentences at the end of this section on page 28 most useful for quick and accurate diagnosis of letter faults.

Marking each other's work makes pupils realise how difficult it is to read poor handwriting. This leads to an understanding of why people criticise *their* writing. This technique teaches self criticism but you must make sure when using it that sensitive pupils are not teased about their writing.

You will still have to give time to diagnose individually, and prescribe relevant exercises. Blanket exercises given to the whole class seldom do any good. Boredom soon sets in with those most in need of help. Copying a passage to *improve* your handwriting is even worse. It only repeats and reinforces the incorrect movements that so desperately need altering.

## ■ Stage 3: assessment

You will have been assessing problems from the start as a part of diagnosis. The more experienced you are the less you will need a checklist.

However comprehensive a checklist you have, it can be of only limited help in many situations. There are many problems that can only be judged on an individual basis. Take a typical example; whether or not to change an older pupil to cursive. A high-achieving eleven-year-old must be encouraged to join up but you will not succeed unless you can persuade the writer of the benefit of the exercise. You will need to explain that initially joined-up will be less neat and not necessarily faster. However, with practice the resulting speed will make all the effort worthwhile. The writing will be more mature.

Dealing with the same problem with a low-achieving fifteen-year-old is quite another thing. It might be pointless and counter-productive to attempt to alter a clear print in this situation. No checklist can help you with that assessment.

When I write in This ontig I can't read it to learn my notes.

*Fast writing*

This is the way I write so that I can read it.

*Slower writing*

This is a good time to think again about speed. It might be useful to see how much faster pupils can write as they improve but can this ever be a real indication of success? Speed alone ignores too many of the other aspects of writing. A simple test against the clock would show if the pupil's writing speed had increased since the last test, but legibility is just as important as speed, and it will not measure that. A more efficient movement can be used to make writing easier to read. Some older pupils actually have to be persuaded to write more slowly. There is a delicate balance between the speed and the legibility of handwriting. Go too far in either direction and you upset this balance.

## Assessment of improvement

There are two points to consider here: the first is why is it necessary? From the teacher's angle a record of improvement is essential. Not only is it needed for the pupil's sake, but professional satisfaction, research surveys, and quite likely school policy depends on the keeping of methodical records.

From the pupil's angle it is usually desirable to compare 'before and after samples'. It is good for morale to see improvement, and essential in helping to develop self-critical awareness in pupils.

The second point is how to set about it. This time let us start from the pupil's angle. Section 3 has been designed as a series of checksheets, but the whole system is meant to be as flexible as possible. Some pupils will have needed your help at every stage, but others may have enjoyed checking in pairs or groups. The most mature, however, will have skimmed through, extracted the information required, and put it straight into use.

These three levels of pupils will have different requirements when it comes to assessing their improvement. The last group will be quite able to monitor their own progress. Their motivation to increase legibility or speed is enough once they understand the problem. Filling in checksheets is not necessary for them; it would only cause annoyance and frustration. *You* will have to do any assessing yourself for your records. These pupils do not want to be reminded of their previous problems!

The middle group may well profit from and even enjoy assessing and marking their own improvement on specially prepared checklists. They will, however, only need those portions that apply to their specific faults. You alone can judge how much use this technique is to each individual, and how much valuable time should be used for it. It is the first and least mature group that will profit most from formal self marking. This does not mean that they are always the worst writers, but that this method is most likely to appeal to them.

It is essential to keep written samples at every stage for you and your pupil to monitor improvement. Your own common sense will guide you on how practical it is to use elaborate checksheets. An inadequate or inappropriate checksheet is more trouble than it is worth. The difficulty in producing a practical checksheet lies in the complexity of problems that you are likely to encounter.

Checklists, despite their limitations, have their uses at two levels:

1 To help teacher and pupil to assess the situation at the early stages of diagnosis.
2 To help assess improvement.

## Guidelines for designing checksheets

You will need to divide a large sheet of paper into six parts. If you find that you need more space, then spread the subjects on to two sheets. A section for general comments is also useful.

The way you use the first 5 parts of the checksheet is fairly straightforward. Part 6 needs some thought.

---

**Name** --------------------------------------------------------

**Form** --------------------------------------------------------

**Date** --------------------------------------------------------

---

**1 Posture**

Body
Arm
Wrist
Hand position
Paper position

**4 Legibility**

Overall legibility ( scale of 5)

Legibility factors 1 - 12
(Section 3, page 48)

**2 Fingers**

How many?
Which leads
How close to the point?
Angle of finger?
Tension
Hand/arm/fingers
Pressure on pen
Pressure on paper
Tremor
Pain

**5 Joins**

Baseline joins
Top joins
Crossbar joins
Joins to round letters
Overall efficiency

**3 Letter Construction**

Wrong point of entry
Wrong direction of stroke
Strokes added
Strokes omitted
Height differentials
Descenders/Ascenders

**6 General Features**

Slant
Size
Spacing
Speed
Alignment
Unconventional letters
Stylistic exaggerations

Comments:

## Using checksheets

Use of a scale of marking is one way of tackling these aspects of handwriting. Use also for Legibility, part 4.

---

### Slant

This could be measured on a scale of 5.

1  Excessive backward slant.
2  Slight backward slant.
3  Upright.
4  Slight forward slant.
5  Excessive forward slant.

An additional measurement is needed for *consistency*.

### Size

This also needs a scale of 5 plus consistency.

1  Too small.
2  Small.
3  Average.
4  Large.
5  Too large.

### Spacing

This also needs a scale of 5 plus consistency.

1  Too close.
2  Close.
3  Good.
4  Wide.
5  Too wide.

### Speed

This could be marked *approximately* on a scale of 5.

1  Very slow.
2  Slow but adequate for the writer's needs.
3  Fast enough for all needs.
4  Very fast.
5  Too fast for legibility.

**Alignment, unconventional letters** and **stylistic exaggerations** require specific observations.

---

## Checksheets for pupils

Pupils will not necessarily need to check the first two sections that deal with their writing posture. The other sections may not be relevant in every case either. Pupils need only a checksheet that shows their specific category of fault. Here is an economical suggestion. Have individual sheets that cover one section of the teacher's checksheet at a time, to be used as appropriate. Even within a specific section not all points will be relevant to each student. Only the four most common faults should be printed on the pupil's checksheets. The rest should be blank for their own faults to be filled in. This gives you real flexibility.

## Marking

You need a marking system that is flexible enough for both you and your pupils. The way you mark will also vary, at different stages.

At the observation level the teacher will only want to record errors. The pupil may use the checksheet in a different way; to learn self-criticism. Marking those points that are satisfactory as well as those that are wrong is a more positive approach, particularly for the insecure child.

At the second stage when you are assessing improvement, a different system of marking will be needed for some aspects of handwriting. It is the consistency of each element that you have changed that contributes to the quality of the reformed hand. A sliding scale of perhaps five or six marks might help you to judge the consistency of slant, spacing, size or even joins. There are two kinds of consistency: short term when you are measuring it in an exercise, and long term.

You will need to work out a system to monitor progress over a period of at least several weeks after retraining.

In the end, a complete quantitative analysis of improvement may be almost impossible.

# ■ Test sentences

These test sentences can be used in several ways:

1 To help you make a quick diagnosis of letter faults when you are teaching a group.
2 To confirm an individual diagnosis.
3 To use as practice after diagnosis.
4 To help you to assess improvement.

These sentences are only suggestions. You or your pupils can invent other ones.

1 To correct o that goes round the wrong way (joined or separate letters).

> You too could cook good food from our cookery book.

2 Leaving strokes off n m r and u (joined or separate letters).

> Can many animals run round in time to music? Winning a running race is fun. Slamming my door jammed it. Sorry about the hurry, the curry is ready.

3 Adding strokes on to v and w (joined or separate letters).

> As we were very weary we were waving farewell. Five vowels will vary.

4 Letter heights for ascending strokes (joined or separate letters).

> The fat thick necked bottle filled half full did better than all the thin little bottles.

5 Letter heights for descending strokes (joined or separate letters).

> Try jogging gently, enjoying yourself, or fly along, play badly, gasp off the field.

6 Simple joins from the base.

> Run up the hill to the mine then hunt in the little tin hut. The minimum limit.

7 Top joins from o r v and w.

> Our two rowers vary, so we try rowing well for records in wind or rough waves.

8 Crossbar joins from f and t.

> Do fill five full fresh mugs for afternoon food. Office coffee is free after four. Will the better train standing at platform two start today at ten thirty three?

9 Joins to round letters c a d g q and o.

> A damaged stage ladder can mean added danger for active actors and dancers.

10 For simplifying or practising s and k.

> Please pass us some sausages as Susan missed us because she was serving someone else. Jack knocked the bucket and the wicked black donkey kicked back.

11 For b/d reversal.

> A bumpy bed is bad, but a hard board would be a bad bed too.

# 3

# Specially for pupils

# ■ So you're having trouble with your handwriting

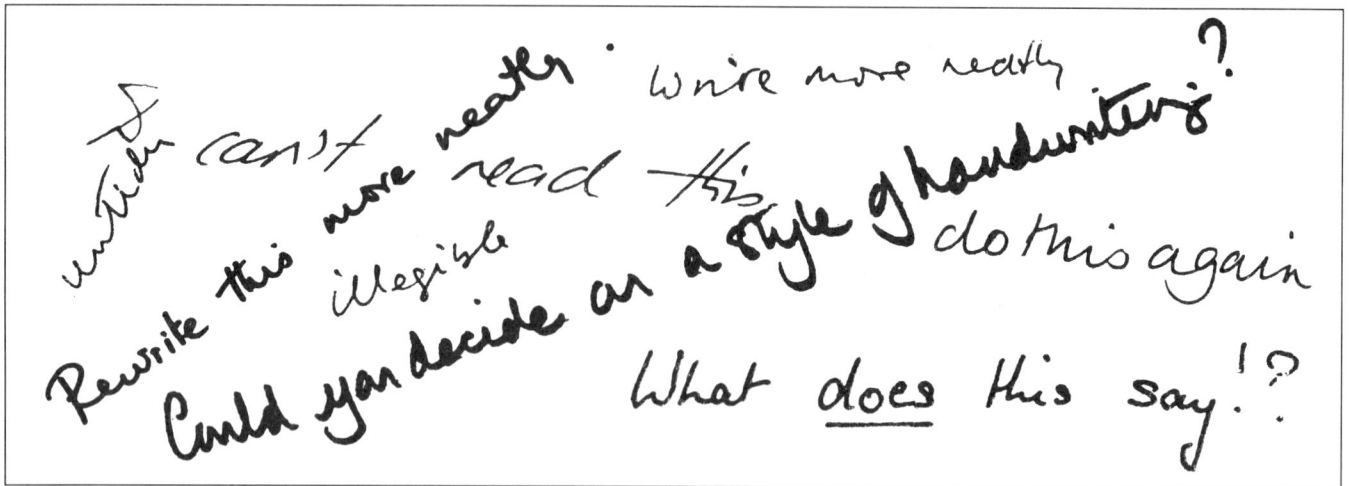

*[handwritten text]:* writer can't write more neatly? Rewrite this more neatly read this illegible Could you decide on a style of handwriting do this again What does this say!?

## You can read it; why can't they?

Do people keep saying that they cannot read what you have written? Other people judge you by your writing but they look for individuality as well as neatness. Good writing must of course be legible but it should flow and have some character.

You do not need the same standard of handwriting all the time. It must be extra good if you are writing a special letter, but when you are writing a quick list for yourself it can be really rough. For note taking and examinations speed is the most important thing and for this you need an in-between standard.

Handwriting is for communicating, not only while you are at school, but also for the rest of your life. If there are any real problems it is worth getting things right now.

## ■ How these sheets can help

Some so-called handwriting problems have little to do with the letters themselves. Read pages 30–42 and you will understand why. Pages 43–63 deal with letters. Pages 64–72 explain themselves. Called 'Spot your own mistakes', some of you may find them the most useful sheets of all.

Handwriting needs to be automatic to leave your mind free to think about other things. You want to concentrate on what you are writing, not what your hand is doing. To get to this level you need proper training. If you've missed out earlier on, these sheets give you another chance. Half the problem is understanding what is wrong. Putting it right may be easier than you think.

## First, ask yourself these questions

1 Is my handwriting worse when under pressure?
2 Does it hurt me to write?
3 Is it so slow that I never get enough done?
4 Is it so fast that it looks sloppy?
5 Is it just *my* writing that is bad? What about other people's?
6 Is it worth all the effort to improve things?
7 Ask yourself these questions again when you have finished the exercises.

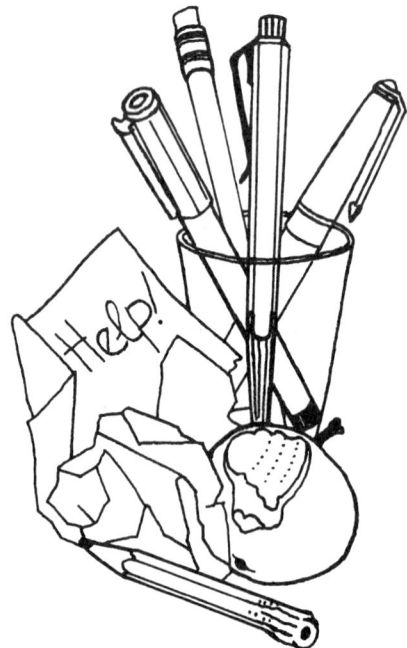

# Before you even start to write

## It really helps if

1 You can see what you are doing.

2 Your desk is the right height for you.

3 Your desk has a good surface.

4 Your paper is in the best position for you.

5 Your pen suits both your hand and your writing.

6 You hold your pen in a way that lets your fingers move freely.

7 You try to keep your desk clear and tidy.

The chair is too low so this boy's shoulders are hunched. He has to twist his hand to see what he is writing.

Two cushions solved this problem. When he was high enough his hand could straighten and his writing flow.

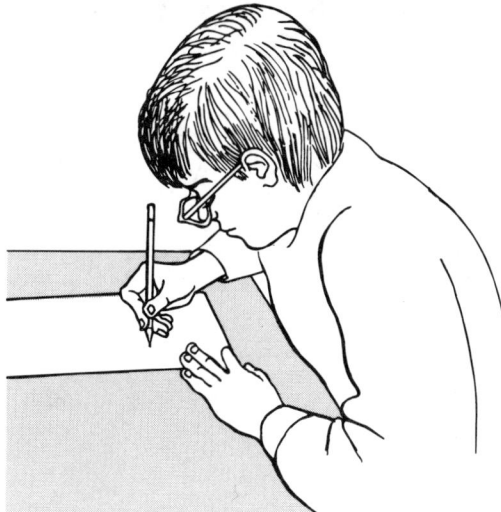

When the desk height is correct, arms are supported and shoulders relaxed. All this helps handwriting.

# ■ What to do about it, and why

**1** If you are right-handed, try to have the light coming from the left. If you are left-handed have the light coming from your right or you'll be working in the shadow of your hand.

**2** Make sure that you can sit comfortably. If your chair is too low you will be hunched up, with your chin almost on the desk. If your chair is too high or the table too low, then you may end up sitting sideways because there is no room for your legs.

**3** Rough desks leave dents in the paper and make your writing jerky. Plastic desks are often too hard. Write on a pad of paper or rest on something that will give slightly.

**4** If you are right-handed, your paper should always be to your right side. If you are left-handed it should be over to your left. This lets your arm move freely as you write and stops you twisting your wrist to see what you are writing. Once the paper is over to the correct side you can position it to suit yourself.

**5** Experiment with different types of pens to find out how they affect your writing and your comfort.

**6** See pages 34–37 for details of penhold.

**7** If there is too much junk piled up on your desk, you may find yourself twisted over to one side because that is the only flat space for your paper. Remember, a right-hander will need space to the right and a left-hander space to the left.

This table is too low and the chair is too small. Together they force the writer to sit sideways. It is awkward and often painful to sit in this position.

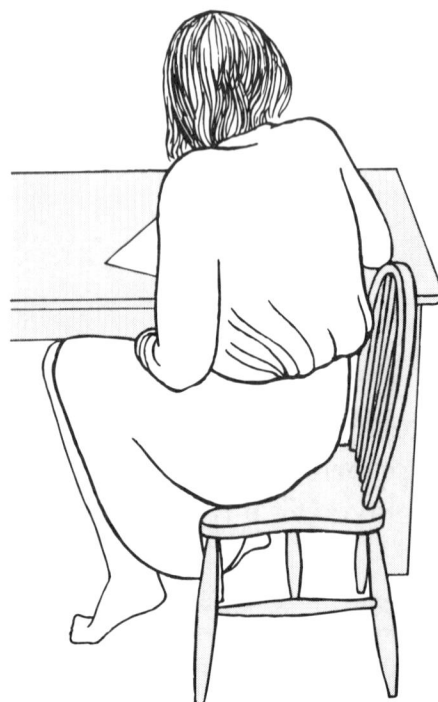

© JOHN MURRAY HELPING WITH HANDWRITING

# ■ Relax and your writing will improve

There is tension in all our lives, at home and at school. When the stress gets really bad, this will show in your writing. Then you may be criticised for bad writing or untidiness. You may grip your pen so hard that it hurts you to write. You may be pressing so hard on the paper that your letters go through several sheets. Your hand can *look* quite relaxed, but tension can be stiffening your arm or shoulder. The way you sit can make your muscles tense, or tension itself can make you sit awkwardly. You may sometimes be so worried, angry or frustrated that neither your thoughts nor your writing can flow freely. It is all connected.

You cannot get rid of all the worry and tension in your life, but you can learn to relax when writing.

1 *Uncross* your legs.

2 Relax your hunched shoulders.

3 Shake your hand until it feels floppy.

4 Take a couple of deep breaths.

Think about how you sit. These three all need to move the paper so they can sit in a more relaxed way. You will get a stiff neck and aching shoulders if you sit badly.

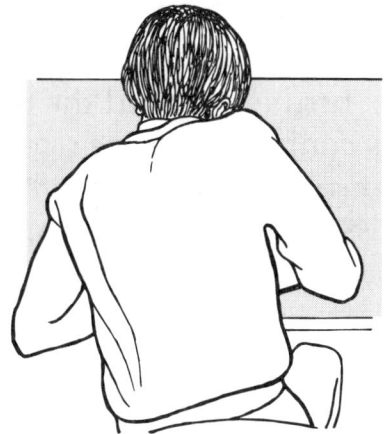

# ■ Penholds

The way you hold your pen affects your handwriting more than you realise. It can make the difference between an aching hand and trouble-free writing. Ask yourself these questions:

**1** Does it hurt me to write for any length of time?

**2** Can I write as fast as I want to?

**3** Does the way I hold my pen distort my letters or restrict my movements?

If the answer to any of these is 'yes', then read on.

The conventional way of holding a pen is called a tripod grip. You put your thumb and first finger gently on either side of the pen and your middle finger underneath. This way everything can move freely as you write. If you have a problem you must look at each part of your grip separately: your finger position, your hand position and your wrist.

## Try these different finger positions

It even makes a difference which finger is nearest the penpoint. When the first finger is in front you can make the quick changes of direction that you need in writing.

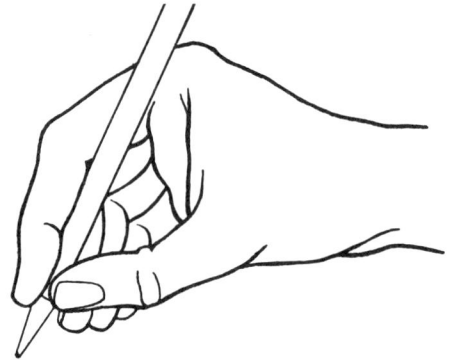

Forefinger in front

The further forward the thumb comes, the less control you have over the pen. You may get a nasty lump where the pen is pressed down on your middle finger.

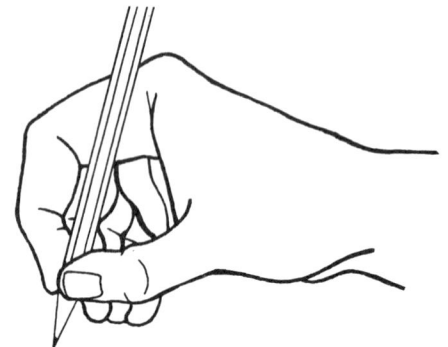

Thumb and finger equal

As your thumb goes even further forward your first finger gets forced up at a sharp angle. This can hurt and you may end up with awkward writing.

Thumb in front

# ■ Hand positions

Do you write with your hand on edge, or is it slightly flattened? The 'hand on edge' way works well if you are relaxed but can cause trouble if you are tense. Under pressure you can tip your hand too far over so your wrist twists. This can hurt. Flatten your hand a little, so that your wrist straightens automatically. This soon stops the pain. Do not go to the other extreme and flatten your hand too much or you will make another set of muscles ache.

The tripod grip works well with a pencil or a fountain pen but not always so well with modern pens. They have to be held more upright to work well. This may be why so many people have unconventional penholds. Some work quite well. Try penhold 7 on the next page. It helps to cure pain and writer's cramp. If your penhold is causing you trouble you must do something about it. First find which part of your hand or arm is strained. Experiment with different positions until your whole hand can relax and move freely.

It may take a while to get your muscles used to a new writing position. Start with some of the relaxing scribbles on page 42 before you try writing long sentences.

When you alter your hand or finger position the slant of your writing can change. Alternatively if you want to change the slant of your writing experiment with your penhold.

This hand is on edge.

This hand is slightly flattened.

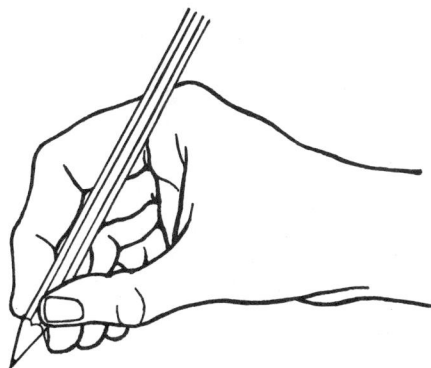

# Unconventional penholds – left hand

Left-handers try to solve their special problems, but do not always succeed.

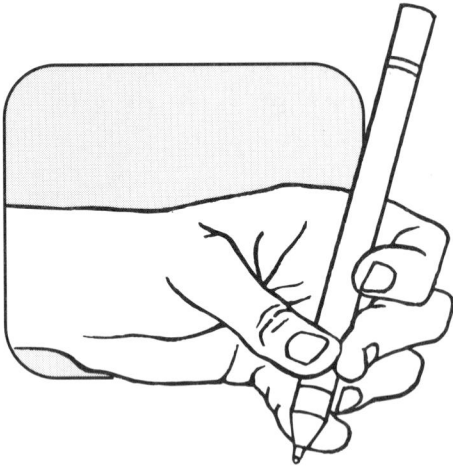

**1** Bad. This restricts and can hurt.

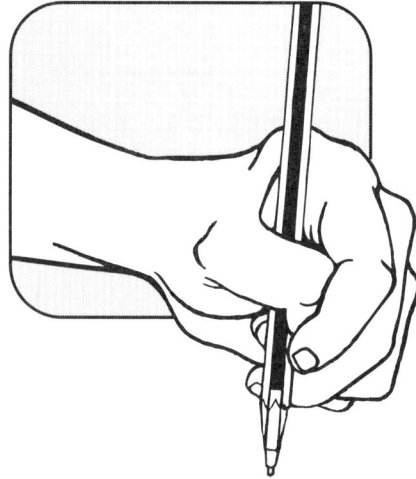

**4** Bad. Fingers cannot move freely.

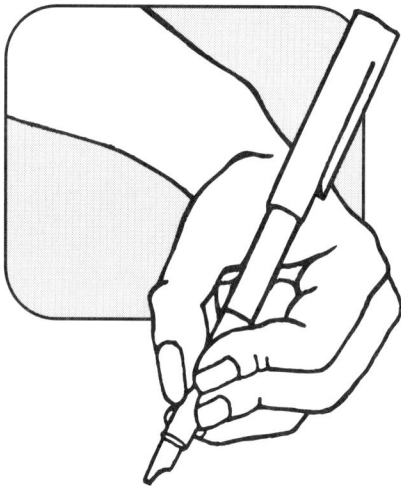

**2** Awkward. Can slow you down.

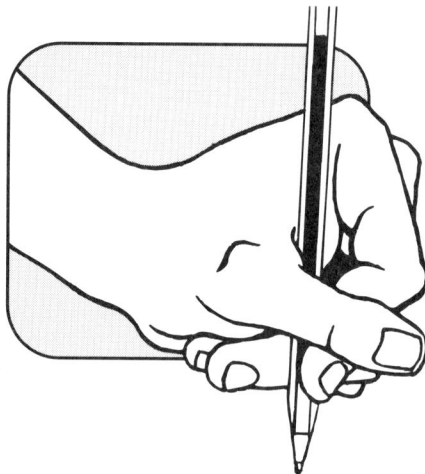

**5** Less control when thumb does no work.

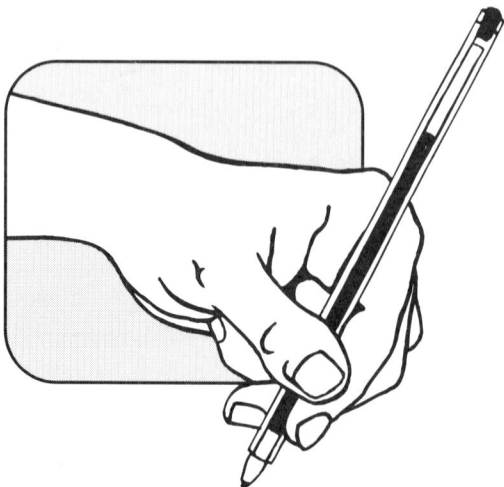

**3** O.K. when relaxed. Lets the pen slant.

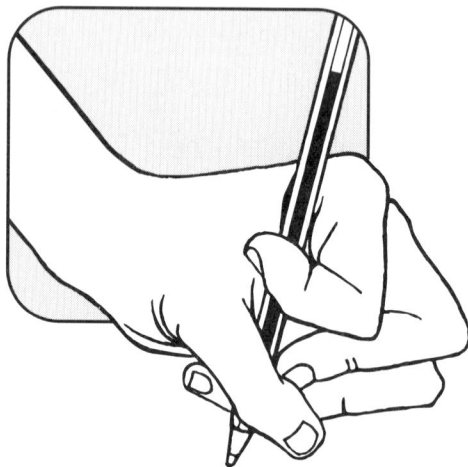

**6** Complicated. Restricts movements.

# ■ Unconventional penholds – right hand

You need to try out these penholds to feel why some work and others do not.

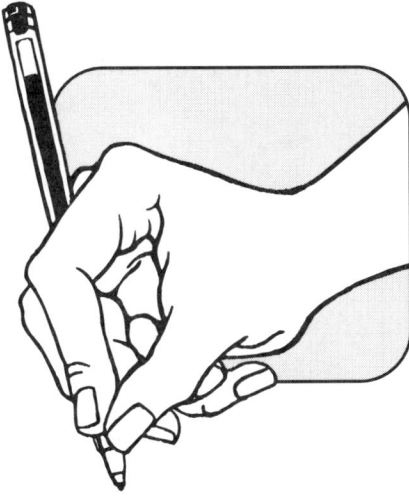

**7** Excellent. Try this alternative.

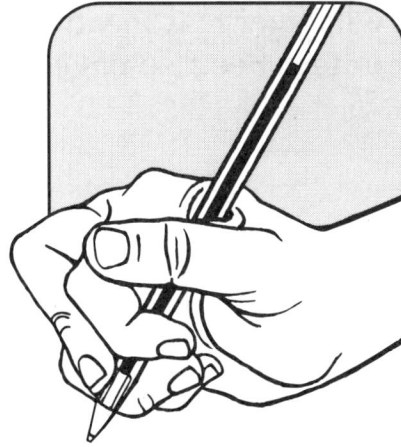

**10** Complex and rather limiting.

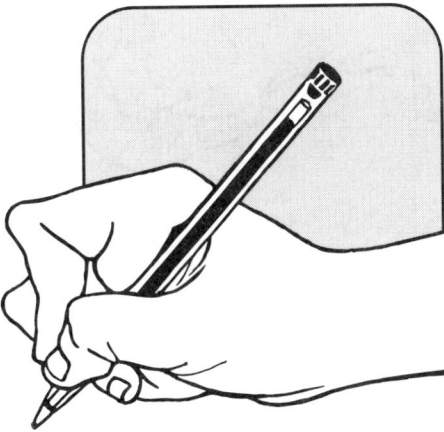

**8** Looks conventional but is tense and painful. Relax.

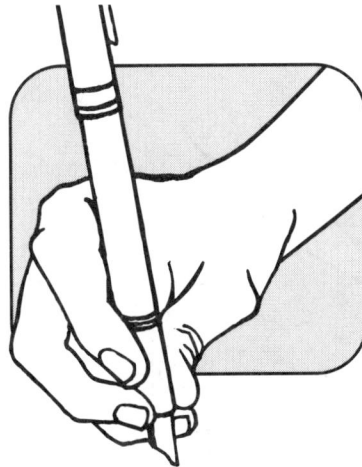

**11** Awkward. Straighten your wrist and relax fingers.

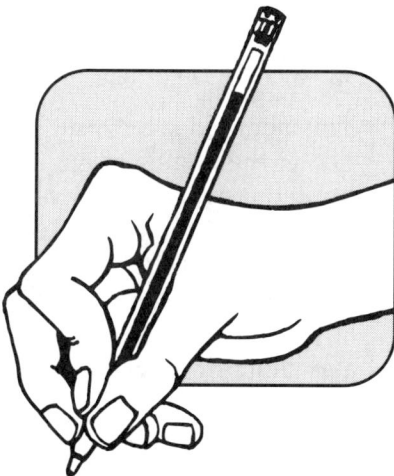

**9** Two fingers can slow you down.

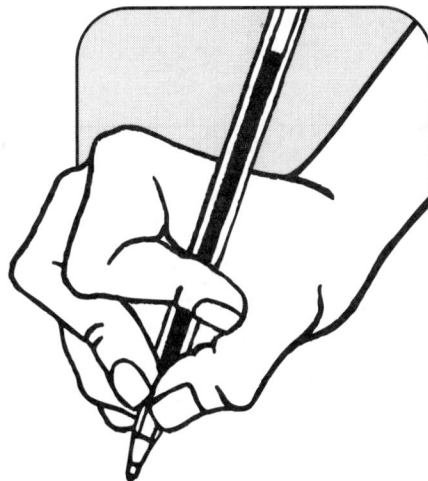

**12** Looks strange but probably works.

# ■ Your hand and your handwriting

The way you hold your pen affects your letterforms. Your whole hand as well as your fingers need to move freely to produce all the different strokes. Your penhold should be relaxed to let you write fast and painlessly. Change penhold, for whatever reason, and you will probably alter the shape and slant of your letters. See also pages 34–37.

This is a tense penhold. The hand is on edge with two fingers stiffly on the pen. The hand cannot move freely enough to make joining strokes. A slow, rather childish printing is the result. Write like this for long and it will hurt.

A complete change of penhold gave immediate relief. The hand is slightly flattened, the fingers relaxed, and the writing now flows. This unconventional but efficient penhold is especially good for those with long fingers.

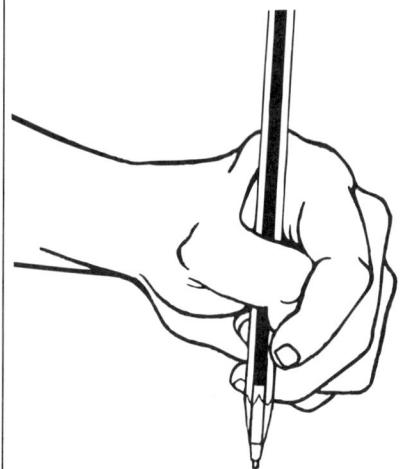

This penhold is a strain. It does not let the fingers move. The limited movement shows in the writing. The hand pushes along the line but cannot go up and down, so there is hardly any difference between the tall and short strokes.

# ▪ Paper position affects how you sit and what you write

Where you place your paper is vital. It influences how you sit, hold your pen and, in the end, what you write. Alter the paper position if it makes you sit awkwardly. Arm muscles and even those in your back are used in writing. They must learn to work together in a new position. It may feel odd at first, but it is worth persisting and it will save real pain and trouble later on.

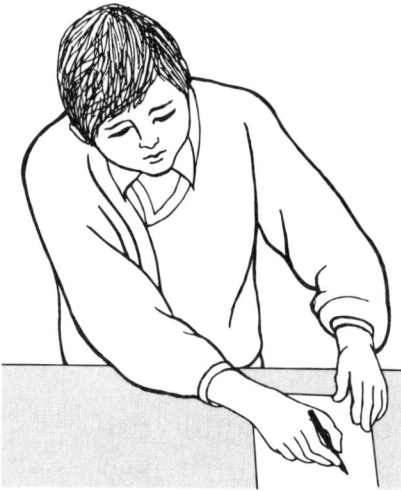

*Birds goes an order: Primate*

*people hate to drive bone-shakers. Lorry because I'm pearall by car. Trains are*

*and bill. Dampier high pitched Kowk roaring sound on birds of prey. habitually dives*

The paper is over to the wrong side. The writer sits badly and cannot see what he is doing. Letters, especially those that join at the top, spread out as he pulls his hand across to make sure that he has got those top joins right.

Some strokes are almost impossible to form with this penhold. Change it or you will have awkward writing. Left-handers need the paper over to the left so they do not have to twist the wrist to see what they are doing.

Some right-handers also twist the wrist and push with the thumb. Once again the result is awkward jerky writing and an aching hand. Moving the paper further to the right will avoid this unnecessary trouble, see page 32.

# ■ Hints for left-handers

Left-handers have different needs from right-handers and these are often overlooked.

1 Sit at the end of the table, or next to a left-hander. You need space to your left side. If you sit to the right of a right-hander, you will bump each other as you work.

2 Find a seat where the strong light comes from your right side, otherwise you will be working in the shade of your own hand.

3 Sit a little higher than your right-handed neighbour. This will help you to see over the top of your hand as you write. Hold your pen a fair distance from the point to help you to see what you are writing.

4 Paper position is *very* important. Put the paper to your left side before you start to slant it. Your arm will move freely. You see what you are doing and you won't smudge.

5 A pen with a smooth point will work best for you. Sharp points dig into the paper and broad edged nibs can be a problem. Fibre tips are good and do not smudge.

6 Some strokes are more difficult for a left-hander. You may want to use slightly different letters from a right-hander, or sequence your strokes differently. See page 57.

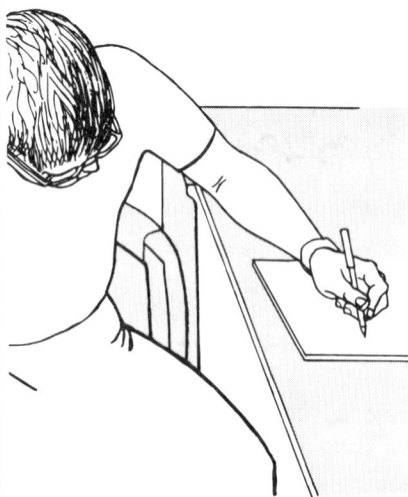

This left-hander had his paper in the wrong position, so he sat sideways.

Now the paper is in the right position he can sit properly at the desk.

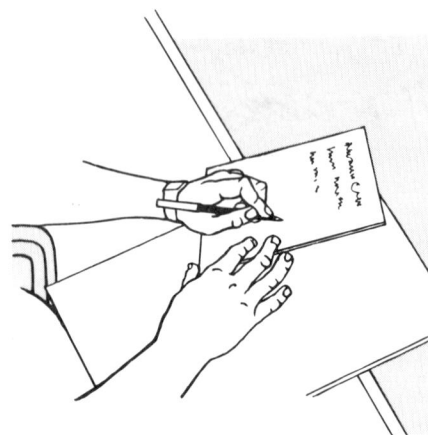

He tried working on a tilted board and liked it. You might like it, too.

# ■ Hand positions for left-handers

When it comes to holding a pen, there seem to be three main hand positions.

1 **Over-the-top** sometimes called **inverted**. The wrist is twisted right round so that the pen comes down from above the line of letters. To change this move the paper over to your left then flatten your hand slightly.

**Advantages:**

You can see what you are doing.
You do not smudge your work.
You can make your letters slant forward easily.

**Disadvantages:**

It is awkward and can hurt you.
It may slow your writing down.
It is difficult to make an undercurve or joining stroke.

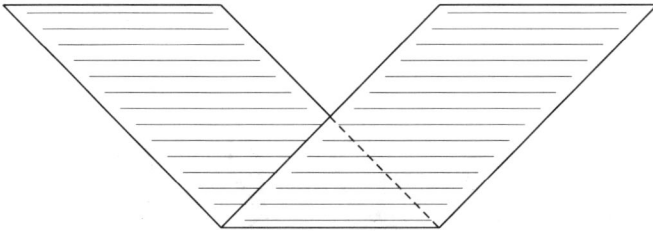

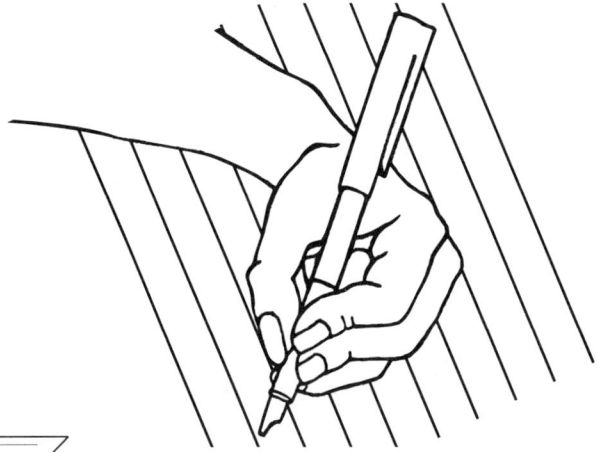

This hand comes from above.

2 **From the side.** *Provided* you make your fingers work and do not push the pen with your whole hand, this can be an effective way to write. Notice above the way the paper can slant either way.

**Advantages:**

You can see what you have just written.
You do not smudge.
Letters are usually upright.

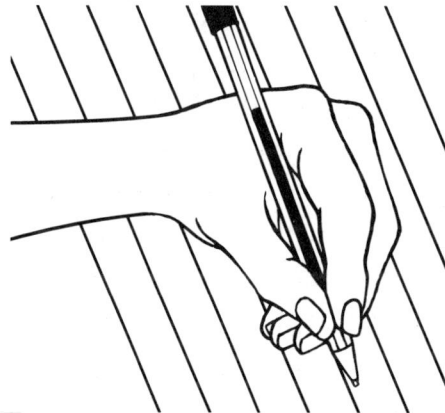

This hand comes in from the side.

3 **From below.** *Provided* you slant your paper and have it well to your left, you should see what you have just written.

**Advantages:**

Fingers are freer so there is less pushing.
It is easier to join up and lets the writing flow.
You are less likely to be criticised!

**Disadvantages:**

Your writing may slope backwards.

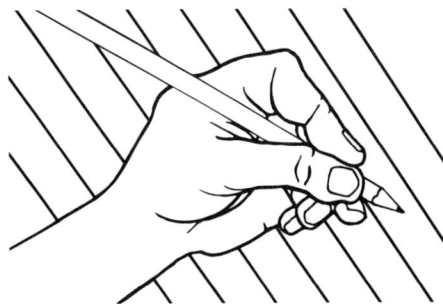

This hand comes from below.

# ■ Relaxing scribbles

Try these relaxing scribbles. They make you loosen up and realise that you can write this way all the time. You can also learn a lot about your writing problems by looking closely at your own efforts.

Can you do both the rounded movements and the joining strokes between the long and short lines? Do you hesitate anywhere? If so, try changing your penhold to help your fingers move more freely. Do you feel that your pen is holding you up, perhaps not moving as smoothly as it ought? If so, it is time you used a more flowing point. What about a fibre-tip pen?

When you started did you press so hard that you could feel the bumpy shapes through the back of the paper? If so, you are using too much force. You do not need to keep turning over the paper to check whether you are improving as you relax. As you put less pressure on the pen the lines get fainter.

Do these relaxing scribbles until your pen is skimming across the page.

# ■ Handwriting is a pattern

Think of written letters as a pattern made up of very few strokes. There are long and short straight strokes, diagonal ones and rounded ones. That leaves only dots and crosses on the letters i, j, f and t.

## Putting letters in family groups

You can separate letters into those using the same stroke and deal with them in family groups. But remember it is meant to be a **moving pattern**. The correct movement is vital. You need to start at the right place and write the strokes in the correct direction. Then when the letters join up they make an understandable pattern. Look at the basic letters below.

These letters are made up of straight strokes **i l t j**

These letters have under arches **u y**

These letters have a downstroke followed by an arch **h n m r b p k**

These letters are all based on c **c a d g q o e**

These letters have diagonal strokes **v w x z** and so does **k**.

These letters start like c then change direction **f s**

*Note: All basic letters start at the top except e and d.*

## How to make up your own exercises

If you have a faulty letter just find another in the same family that you *can* write correctly. Repeat them together a few times. The right one will help the wrong one to move correctly.

## Grouping letters by height

These letters go above the line of writing **b d f h k l**

These letters go below the line of writing **f g j p q y**

These letters do not go up or down **a c e i m n o r s u v w x z**

The letter **t** is taller than **i** but not as tall as **l**

These letters are a useful pair if you are having crossbar problems **t f**

# ■ If the movement is wrong

Wrongly formed letters can make joined up writing almost impossible to read. A smoothly flowing movement leads to more efficient handwriting and is less strain on your hand.

a young man Find out about murder and under

Many of these letters are wrongly formed. See the o, a, n, m, d and u. They must be corrected before they can join properly. This writer would need to go right back to the groups of basic letters on page 43 and start from the beginning again.

### Here are the usual mistakes

1 Starting at the wrong place.

O leads to *aa* instead of *oo*
d leads to *ded* instead of *ded*

2 Going round the wrong way.

O leads to *oo* instead of *oo*
g leads to *go* instead of *go*

3 Leaving strokes out.

m leads to *hm* instead of *him*
r leads to *art* instead of *art*

4 Adding strokes on.

u leads to *win* instead of *win*
u leads to *eue* instead of *eve*

Check the points on these pages against your own writing or get a couple of friends to do it for you.

# ■ Are you leaving strokes out ?

Letters that have a stroke missing are misleading. You must deal with them.

This u cannot join properly because the final downstroke is missing.

used much. Just up

First practise u and y together. These exercises will help.

uy uy up up us us

The vital downstroke is missing from r. The word 'around' looks like 'wound'.

bird char n around

Practise h and r saying to yourself 'down up and over'.

hr hr hr ir ir ir ar ar

The first stroke is left off n m and r in 'animal training'. The joined up m looks like n.

animal taing

Practise h and n saying to yourself 'down up and over'.

hn hn hm hm hnm

No downstrokes again on m and n. It is more confusing still with mature handwriting.

navy moderate

Practise all these three combinations.

hn hm hr hn hm hr

## ■ Letter heights are important

Did you know that the top half of letters give you most of the information that you need? Cover over the bottom half of the sentence below. You will find that you can still read it.

## show that this rule does work
## show that this rule does work

hnty — ascender / descender

You also need the strokes that go below the line. They are called descenders. Together the different heights give the word a shape. This makes your handwriting easier for other people to recognise and read.

Here are some letter patterns. They help you to notice how letters that look alike can have different heights.

i l t u y j h n f
a g d q b p k

Here are some words to practise. Make their shape clear by giving the letters adequate ascenders.

bag joy lift hat

little quickly fluffy

When handwriting is joined up the different heights are even more important in making your writing legible. Now that you understand why, it becomes easier to make any necessary alterations to your letters.

# ■ If the letter heights are wrong

Letter heights must be correct or your writing will be difficult to read. This is because fluent readers do not go from letter to letter but take in the whole shape of the word at one time.

These sequences will help to correct the letter heights.

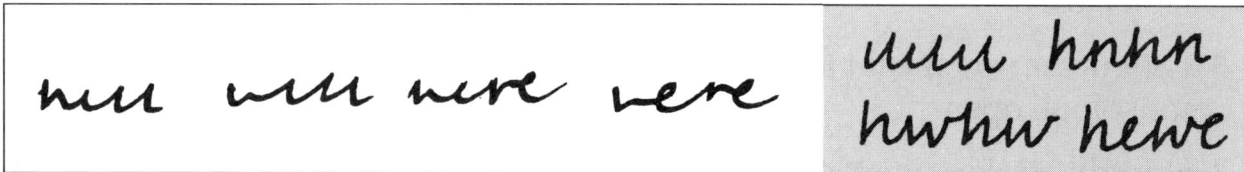

This says 'hill will' and 'here were'. Short h and bad joins from the w muddle the words.

Here the letters that should go below the line cause the trouble, j, y and p.

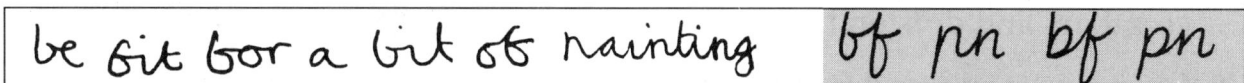

This says 'be fit for a bit of painting' but f is too short and can get confused with the open b. The p is too short. It looks like n.

You can simplify the letter f but it must go below the line or it looks like a t. Notice the short h.

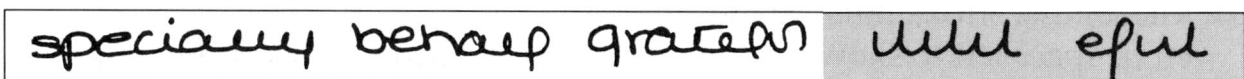

f and l are too short. A stroke left off the u in 'grateful' makes matters worse.

# ■ Twelve rules of legibility

## These points apply to separate letters as well as joined up letters

1 Letters must be the correct height in relation to each other.

2 Letters meant to be closed must look closed.

3 Letters that are meant to be open must look open.

4 Straight strokes must look straight.

5 Curved strokes must look curved.

6 Parts of letters meant to be joined together must be joined.

7 Loops and arches must appear, also crossbars and dots on i.

8 Overcurves and undercurves must differ.

9 Space letters so that it is clear where one letter ends and the next begins.

## These points apply to joined up letters

10 Finish one letter before starting the next.

11 The joining stroke must be indicated or space left to show where one letter ends and the next begins.

12 The joining must not distort a letter so that it looks like another, or suggest an extra letter.

# ■ Why and when to join up

### Reasons for joining once you're used to it

**1** It is usually faster.

**2** It is more mature.

**3** It helps the flow of writing and this also makes it easier for your hand.

**4** It spaces your writing as well as joining it.

### Reasons against joining if you are not used to it

**1** Sometimes it is less legible.

**2** At first it may not be so neat.

**3** It may be slower until you have practised.

You do not need to join all your letters all the time. Your hands need a rest, and a chance to move along the line too. Continuous joining of long words makes writing slower, not quicker. Start with the joins that come easiest to you and join **when it is comfortable.**

# ■ Simple joins have groups

| | |
|---|---|
| Letters that can join from the base | i l t u h m n a d c e k |
| Letters that can join from the top | o r v w |
| Letters that can join from the crossbar | f t |
| Letters that can join with loops at speed | f g j y q |
| Letters that are joined over the top and back | a c d e g o q |
| Letters that you can join or leave unjoined | b p s x z q |

## ■ Start joining in easy stages

The first group of letters with joins at the base:  i l u h m n.

If you have always printed straight letters, then you might enjoy feeling what it is like to write flowing, separate letters like those above.

First try letters in patterns.  It is really easy this way.

*ilil unin*

ililiil inininin hnhnhn

mumu nmhnm nhuy

ill hill mill in my mum

lit hit hunt minimum

Then try words like mill, hunt, hum, hill, nut, etc. Write them faster and faster and you will soon find that you are joining up automatically.

*un my tin hut it hit my hill minimum*

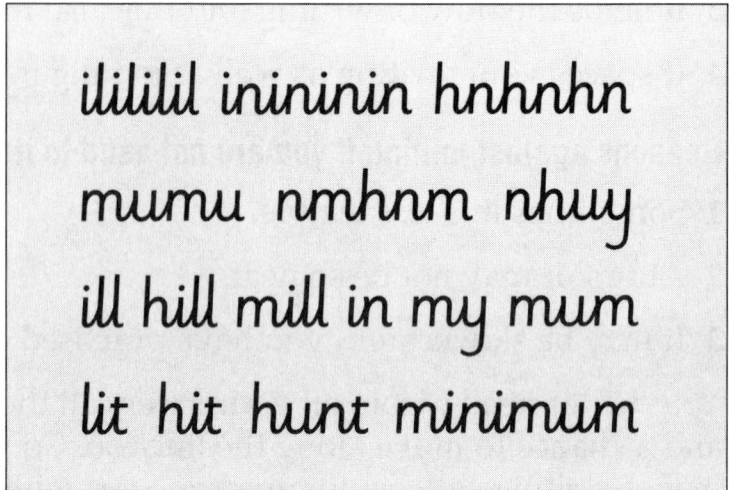

### Check the up stroke at the base of your letters

1  If it is too steep and jagged then your letters are too close together and get muddled up.

2  If it is too shallow then your writing becomes  too spread out. Your joining stroke *spaces* your letters, so try to find a middle way. Then your writing will look even and be easy to read.

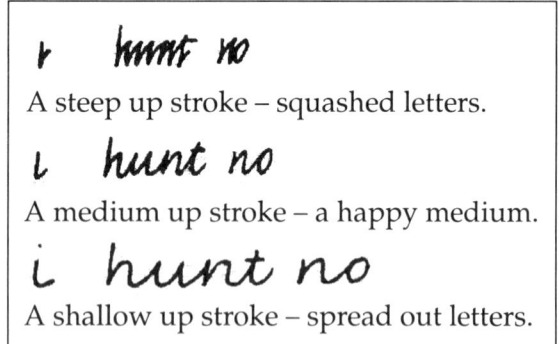

*hunt no*
A steep up stroke – squashed letters.

*hunt no*
A medium up stroke – a happy medium.

*hunt no*
A shallow up stroke – spread out letters.

Do not stop in the middle of short words to dot your i and cross your t.

Write *little* then *little*. *thin* then *thin*.

You should write all of a short word without stopping and then you can go back to finish off the bits. See page 53 for crossbar joins.

# Top joins are great time-savers

## The letters that join from the top are o r v and w

Try a line of looped o s to get used to the feeling. Do it faster and faster.

ooooooo ovovovo
orororo owowow
row vow own room
word wool horror
ol of wh rk owe ore

Make patterns and some words. Forget about being neat.

Notice the joins go up to tall letters and down to e.

These words show how top joins vary with different styles of writing.

two vowel wood room
row work own kon

See what happens to the top of the r. Practise yours before each vowel.

worry rat red earn
ran red rim rod run

You need not join r to the next letter.

These samples are better unjoined.

earn our person
earn ours person

# ■ Joins to the round group of letters

The letters that have reverse joins to them are a c d g q and o. These joins work best with oval slanting writing. With fat letters the join has to go over the top and back. Try the examples below to see what happens. A penlift may be better than an awkward join.

Try these letter patterns first.

*acaca adada agaga*
*cecece dedede aqaq*
*no do go dad laced*
*added caged jagged*

Then try these words.

These fat letters have uneconomic joins.

*cacaca no cacle*

These pointed letters have efficient joins.

*ad ag ad dag gad add*

These round letters have looped joins.

*adadad how poor*

This is a good solution to a bad join.

*hra bd had had world*

It is important to keep your c's round enough.

*chchch church*

These letters are better unjoined.

*eel uge ed uge*

# ■ Crossbar joins

Your crossbar must be at the right height, not too high and not too low.

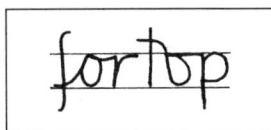

*for top*

Too low    Too high

Try crossbar joins to each vowel in turn, then th. The combinations tt, ff come next then short words.

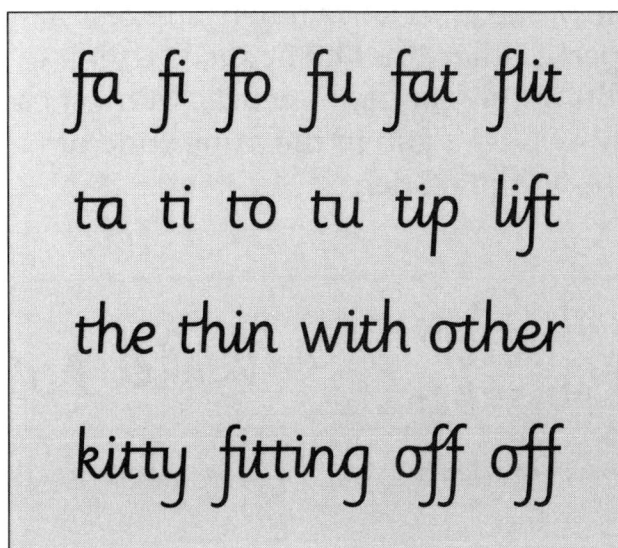

*fa fi fo fu fat flit*
*ta ti to tu tip lift*
*the thin with other*
*kitty fitting off off*

These words show how top joins vary with different styles of handwriting. See what happens to the top of the r. Practise your joins before each vowel in turn.

*the then that for offer*

*for the to the town*

**Beware:** Wrongly constructed letters do not join properly at all.

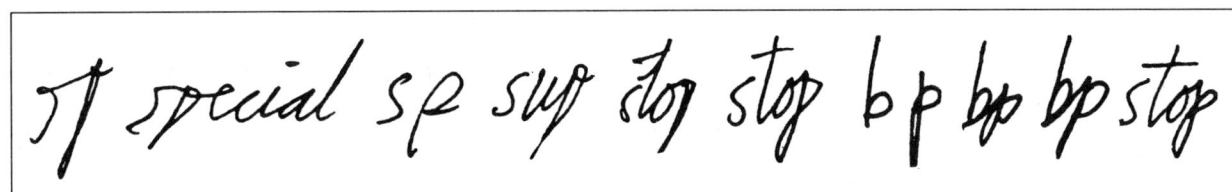

*rf special sp sup stop stop b p bp bp stop*

This s starts at the wrong place. The p starts correctly but then goes mad. It was easy to alter the s but p took longer. The b helped p to move properly.

# ■ Repairing bad joins

Joins must not wander too far up or down, suggest another letter or lose one. Remember that joins are there to help your writing flow and mature. If they end up making your writing difficult to read then something must be done. Some of the joins shown here suggest that the writer was never taught properly, others that he or she is trying to join too much and needs to take a penlift in the middle of words. In most cases the writing has been corrected to show how a join in the same style of writing would work and make words clearer to the reader.

| | | |
|---|---|---|
| *art when* / *art when* | *hole hole* | *wound follow* / *would follow* |
| Bad joins to tall letters. | Do not slide over the top. | Wrong joins muddle words. |

| | | |
|---|---|---|
| *Every two* / *Every two* | *live well* / *live well* | *wood waded* / *wood waded* |
| Top joins must not droop. | Joins look like an extra letter. | Strokes lost by joining. |

| | | |
|---|---|---|
| *when she brushed* / *when she brushed* | *away days* / *away days* | *cat sat* / *cat sat* |
| h slides carelessly into the next letter. | A stroke missing between a and y. | Finish letters properly. |

*see servant* *glasses as* *fish is*

Do not pull the letter s out of shape. Simplify it or do not join at all. This may be quicker too.

# ■ Fast writing and slow writing

Have you noticed what happens to your writing when you speed it up? If your slower writing does not join much it often joins more at speed. On the other hand if you join every letter when you write slowly then some letters may be unjoined when you write faster. All this is good. It is also good if you find ways of simplifying your letters or joins to help you to write faster.

This writing became more relaxed as it got faster. Notice how the word 'the' altered.

This writing gets much more mature at speed. It will get more organised with practice.

This girl's example explains it all. Some writing does not speed up and needs to be simplified.

You can go too fast. This writer must slow down. He is going so fast that he cannot control the s in 'these' or complete the k in 'strokes.'

Don't cut too many corners at speed, 'better known' reads as 'better brown'.

# ■ Looping at speed

Some letters will start to loop automatically when you write faster. It often pays to loop a descender at the beginning of a word, and sometimes in the middle. It is a waste, however, to put a loop on the final letter.

*jog  jog  jogging  ing*

You often loop some of your descenders when you write fast, but not necessarily the final one. It can be a waste of time.

# ■ Fast personal joins

Now your writing is ready to speed up. Your joins are becoming automatic, but you may not always use the same ones. These sets of words on the right will show you why.

You can find one form of a letter at the beginning of a word and another in the middle or at the end. You plan several letters in advance when you are writing fast. The shape of a letter, therefore depends on what was written before and what comes next. Your hand may need a penlift after writing several complex movements. You start again with a simpler letter, so even double letters are not always identical.

This is the kind of variation that makes handwriting interesting.

Letters alter shape according to where they are in the word. Your letter t f or s at the start of a word is likely to be different to one at the end. Try it. Double letters can vary even more and are very personal. You may like your friend's double fs but you probably won't be able to copy them!

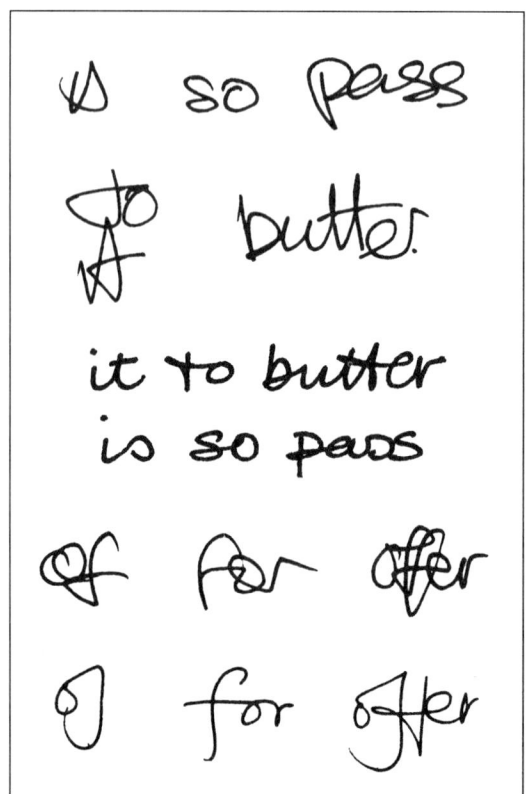

*is  so  pass*

*to  butter*

*it to butter*

*is so pass*

*of for offer*

*of for offer*

# Letters and joins for left-handers

Some of the movements involved in writing our alphabet are awkward for left-handers. Try this simple test: draw two straight lines in opposite directions. Most left-handers find drawing from right to left far easier. That is why almost all left-handers cross their f and t from right to left. Crossbar joins may well feel strange.

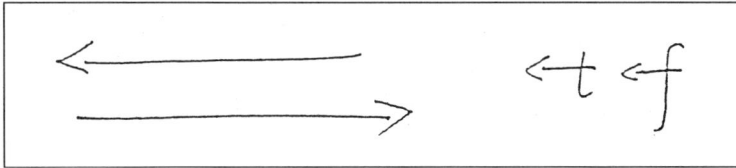

A right to left line is easier for most left-handers.

Retracing the stroke may make crossbar joins easier.

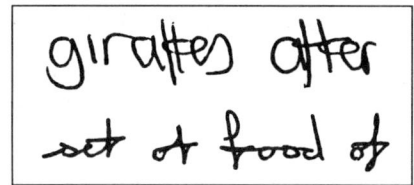

You will find it easier to retrace the stroke up the f or t to make a crossbar join. You can try slightly different letterforms to make use of your most comfortable movement. Start your t with a right to left crossbar. This works well at the beginning of a word.

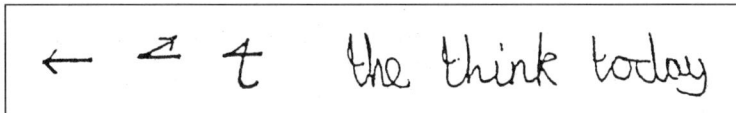

Left-handers find ingenious ways to deal with crossbars.

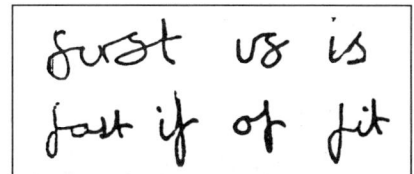

A different way to start the letter t.

The letters f and s can be awkward because they change direction in the middle. Try simplifying them. Experiment until you find something that suits you.

Simplifying the letters f and s.

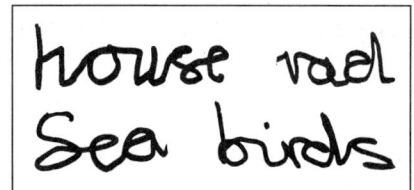

If you have to push uphill to join to round letters you might find it easier not to bother. Lift your pen more often and your handwriting might be easier to read.

Awkward joins to round letters.

Changing your hand position can also make things better. See page 35.

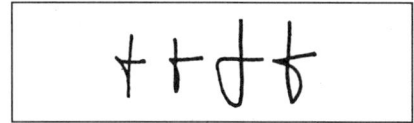

# ■ How far can you go with letters?

## Keep the basic shape of your letters conventional

You do not want to have exactly the same writing as everyone else but if you want people to be able to read it easily then you have got to keep within certain limits. As well as the list on page 48 there are other things to watch.

Adults do not read every letter of every word. They scan the general shape of the word, but when they come to a mixture of unusual shapes they have to stop and puzzle it out. Simple letters can be personalised and still be recognisable at speed, but unusual letter shapes cause confusion.

You need to keep the identity of each letter, so do not lose the differences between n and u.

The letter i should have a dot and not a large circle. It can get so exaggerated that they suggest another letter.

Those squiggles that are used to decorate g and y are also best kept for personal correspondence. They may be fun, but distract the reader and make your hand travel in the wrong direction. An economical movement looks better and works better, too.

Loops can get out of hand and your handwriting can end up looking like knitting.

**Some awful examples**

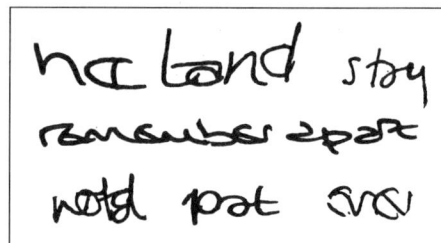

a and e get the worst treatment.

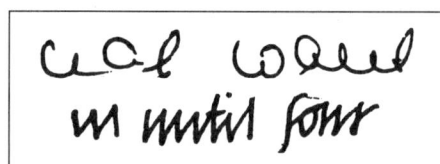

u and n arches must look different.

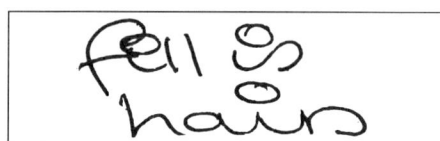

Circle on i looks silly.

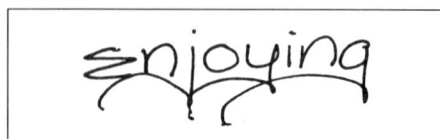

Squiggles are confusing.

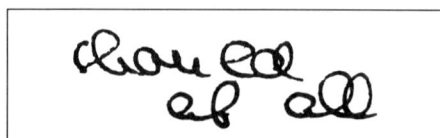

Muddled loops. This says 'should at all', believe it or not !

# ■ Slant

The most practical letters slope slightly forward, join easily and speed up well. But like everything else, slant is a personal matter. You need a consistent but not too pronounced angle for efficient legible handwriting. Upright letters may work well for you, but even then you may find that they tilt forward a little when you go really fast.

Many left-handers and some right-handers have writing that slopes slightly backwards. This seems to annoy some people but as long as the backward slant is slight and consistent it should not slow you down too much or affect legibility. Too much slant, either backwards or forwards, does make writing hard to read. Try to avoid this.

Handwriting that slants in different directions is not only distracting to read but suggests that the writer may be confused too. If your writing is a mixture of backward, upright and forward strokes then try to make up your mind which slant suits you best. Practise until one angle becomes natural. You can rule yourself some slant-lines for a while to encourage regularity.

*and honey my smile*

Whatever angle, be consistent.

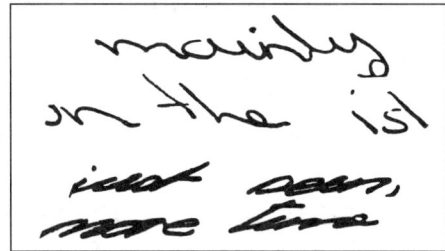

*mainly on the isl iust seen, more time*

Too much slant is hard to read.

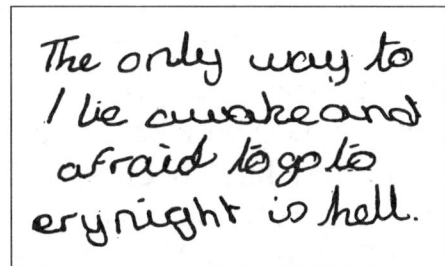

*The only way to I lie awake and afraid to go to ery night is hell.*

A mixture of slants is distracting.

The way you use your hands affects the slant of your letters. To alter slant you will have to alter the angle of your hand.

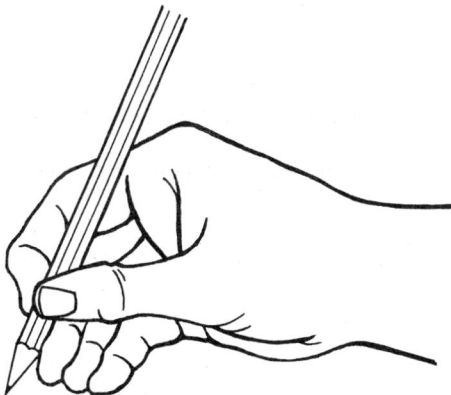

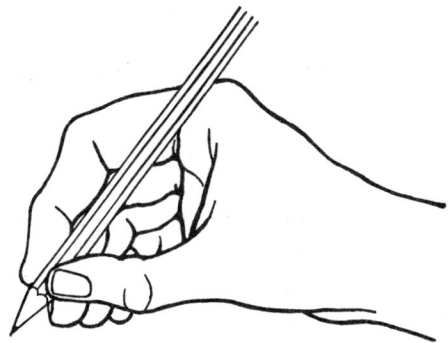

Now look at page 35. It gives further explanation of how your hand position can affect the slant of your writing.

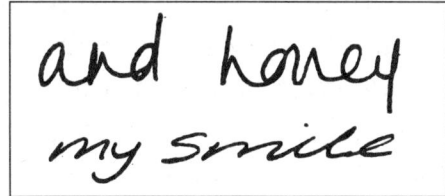

# How much space is 'enough'?

It is difficult to give rules about spacing joined up letters. They must hold together as words but each letter must be separately recognisable. You need to space your words out enough to be able to tell where one ends and the next begins. That is obvious, but how much space is *enough*?

Large, loosely spaced letters need more space between words than smaller and more compact ones. The space between words varies with the size of letter and width of joining stroke. That is why it does not work too well when people with tiny writing try to make it more legible by leaving large gaps between words. It only breaks the page up and makes matters worse.

The space of an o of the same size as the writing is sufficient for **print script**.

For **joined** writing, you may need the space of an o with enough room for a joining stroke on each side. It is all related to your writing, but when the spaces are too wide white patches distract the reader. Some of you may remember being taught to use a thumb or finger to space between letters. At five years old you may have been told to place it on the paper. Later on you used it as a mental spacer. Forget that lesson. Your thumb has grown with age and your writing has shrunk. Your spaces would be huge.

*neatoprintoscript*
*neat print script*

*withojoinedowriting*
*with joined writing*

This fat writing has wide spacing.

Most of the i
the only town

This smaller writing has closer spacing.

living mainly by fishing.
the only town on the is!

This small writing has rather wide spaces.

small island whose inhabi
town on the island als

This spacing is much too wide.

ore and yo
Blut when his
le ren all

# ■ Spiky letters or round letters

Why are there so many differently shaped letters and different kinds of handwriting? It is partly because of what we have been taught. There are so many models and each one is what someone at some time decided the ideal letter shape should be. Teachers know that good, clear writing will help a student get on. They cannot be blamed for trying to get you to write *well* in the conventional sense. However, many people will not follow a conventional model. A very tense person may also be unable to do so. When it comes to style, what one person admires the next person may hate. That is why this book stresses the need for efficient personal handwriting and does not suggest any special model.

A pointed personal italic. This is a decorative style of handwriting and needs a lot of skill to make it work.

> also greatly intrigued by the
> could not read but liked
> would like to know more

A more rounded cursive. This is an example of relaxed left-handed writing. It is pleasant and easy to read but quite different.

> hon of essays
> hed historians
> a condensed

Our handwriting is also part of what we are like ourselves and how our arm and body work. Quite understandably we like our own kind of writing, though sometimes we might like to be a bit better at it! That is where the problem lies. A son who wants to be an artist or perhaps a footballer, is unlikely to have the same writing as a mother who works in a bank. He probably has quite different tastes and interests. A girl who might want to be a designer or perhaps a biochemist, will probably be a different kind of person with different writing from her English teacher. One is not right and the other wrong, they are just different.

## ■ Mixed-up models

There are so many styles taught in our schools it is no wonder that some of you end up in a muddle.

At one extreme there is **italic**. The word italic is meant to describe oval, slightly slanted letters. These letters are often taught with a broad-edged nib. This is supposed to make writing easier, but with some young children their italic ends up being too jagged. Then it is difficult to read.

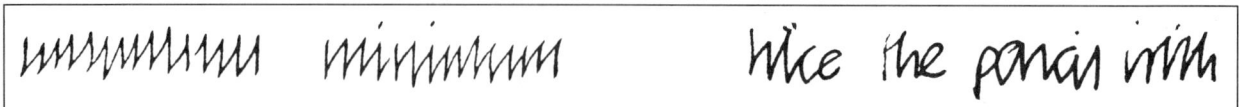

This is 'minimum' upside down, isn't it amazing? Zigzag writing can be difficult to read.

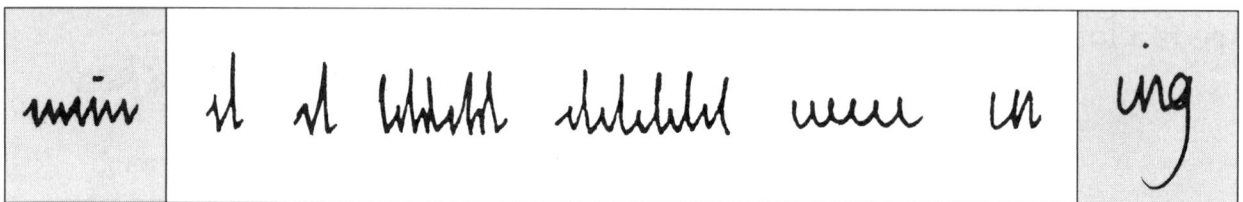

Before          You can exercise your way out of a jagged movement.          After

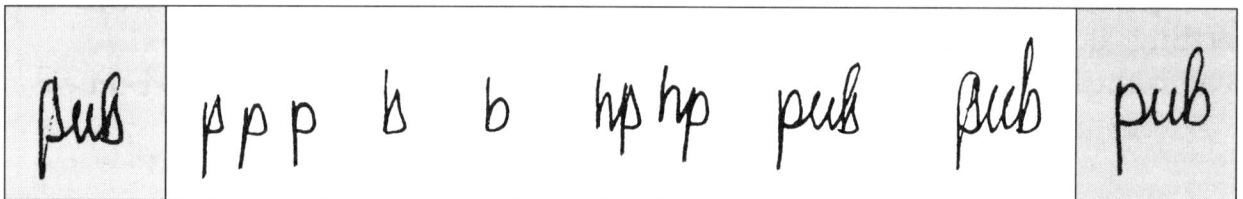

Before.          Loosen up your letters group by group.          After.

Any style can become exaggerated. Look at your writing with this in mind. Have you ended up with a strange assortment of letters? This can happen to anyone who has had to change schools and models several times. The actual shape of your letters and the different angle of joining strokes can cause uneven writing. Divide your letters into family groups as shown on pages 43 and 49, and see if this helps you to sort out a more unified alphabet for yourself.

# ■ Rounded letters

At the other extreme to italic there are rounded, simplified **cursive** models. They are meant to teach five and six year olds to join up easily. They do this job very well – sometimes too well. Some of these children are left for life with the idea that they *must* join all their letters all the time. See page 49.

This is like the model. Every letter joins. It is clear, but slow, and rather childish.

*island made up of by volcanic erupti*

Notice the awkward joins to a o and d. A pen lift would be quicker than joining.

*made land who small*

Some people go back to separate letters when their joins do not work well.

*island whose lies a small rock*

Rounded letters can open out at speed. Narrower writing often works better.

*ring morning*

The simplified letters deteriorate at speed. The open b p and r are worst.

*real places more paintings really.*

*by by ly*

Careless writing mixes n r and p.

b loses its shape and looks like l.

*opposed people*

*by bpbp re*

This p does not do well at speed.

Close b and p and dip the top of r.

# ■ Spot your own mistakes

Have you ever felt that strange feeling when you look at handwriting just like your own? In this part of the book the examples that resemble your own handwriting will be the most useful ones for you. They are meant to help you understand why other people may find your writing difficult to read, even if you can understand it easily. Solutions to familiar looking examples may also work for your own handwriting. Some of the examples may look a bit exaggerated, but they are all real handwriting.

Use the following pages by yourself to help you discover what may be wrong with your own writing. No one can *make* you alter your handwriting, and it is difficult for you to do anything about it until you understand what is worrying the reader about it. Understanding the problem is far more important than doing any exercises, because in the end any alterations have to come from inside yourself.

If you want to alter any part of a letter then you have to alter the way your hand moves to make that letter. Many people forget that learning to write involves training the body in a movement just as training for a sport or ballet, or learning to play music does. Don't be discouraged if it takes some time to alter your handwriting. When you are in the middle of writing an interesting bit of work then you will probably go back to making the same old mistake because you have done it automatically for so long. You cannot worry about your handwriting all the time or you would never get enough written down, however, after a while, whatever you want to alter will become automatic if you really want it to. It is good to know that most of what needs to be done to improve your handwriting can be done by you yourself.

# Different sized letters

Letters that are different sizes make your writing uneven. They get out of line and distract the reader. The most usual culprits are s and k. They are complex letters that have several changes of direction to make in a small space.

s and k are too tall. A more economical movement will help.

Simplify them or practise until they work better for you.

Bad joins make these letters stick out, so lift your pen instead and rest your hand.

More bad joins push your letters out of line. Those to o and s are the worst.

Tension can distort your writing and make your letters vary in size. Relax. See page 33.

You can get careless about the heights of letters if you do not join. See page 47.

## ■ Large writing and small writing

The size of your writing is a personal matter but there are limits. Small writing must be clear and well spaced or it will be hard to read. Tiny writing can be a sign of tension. Relax and it gets larger. Over-large writing gets muddled as the lines mesh together.

### Small writing

Small letters must be clear and well spaced.

> It was most pleasant to stay for dinner. I did enjoy meeting and talking with your family — not that I was able to as much as I'd have liked
>
> island made up of rock formed

Complex or careless writing is illegible when small.

Try to control the size of your letters so that there is space between the lines of writing.

### Large writing

Many of these letters are wrongly formed. Making them larger does not make them any more legible.